W9-ALV-420

BIG CITY FIRE TRUCKS

VOLUME II • 1951–1996

Donald F. Wood & Wayne Sorensen

Dedication

To Chris Cavette, editor of the California Chapter Newsletter of the Society for the Preservation and Appreciation of Antique Motor Fire Apparatus in America.

Some time (and five books) ago, Chris introduced this book's two coauthors because he thought they might have something in common.

© 1997 by

Donald F. Wood and Wayne Sorensen

All rights reserved. No portion of this publication may be reproduced or transmitted in any form or by any means, electronic or mechanical, including photocopy, recording, or any information storage and retrieval system, without permission in writing from the publisher, except by a reviewer who may quote brief passages in a critical article or review to be printed in a magazine or newspaper, or electronically transmitted on radio or television.

Published by

krause publications

700 E. State Street • Iola, WI 54990-0001
Telephone: 715/445-2214

Please call or write for our free catalog of automotive publications. Our toll-free number to place an order or obtain a free catalog is 800-258-0929 or please use our regular business telephone 715-445-2214 for editorial comment and further information.

Library of Congress Catalog Number: 96-76690
ISBN: 0-87341-492-6
Printed in the United States of America

Contents

Preface 4

Introduction 5

Chapter 1: 1951-1960 6

Chapter 2: 1961-1970 53

Chapter 3: 1971-1980 119

Chapter 4: 1981-1990 197

Chapter 5: 1991-Present 290

Bibliography 332

Index by Manufacturer 333

Preface

*I*n 1993, Krause Publications published a book of ours, *American Volunteer Fire Trucks*, which dealt with small-town fire apparatus frequently manned by volunteers. Most of the apparatus covered in that book were outfitted on commercial truck and bus chassis.

In this book, which is actually in two volumes, we look at big city apparatus, with the word big modifying two different words, city and apparatus. Featured in this book are apparatus that one associates with big city, full-time professional departments. Secondly, many of the engines and trucks shown are physically large; in big cities one saw the aerial ladder trucks and water towers that would not be found in small town America. Most of the big city equipment is built by "name" manufacturers and considered as "custom," and carries names such as Pierce or Seagrave. These custom builders also outfitted some commercial trucks. For instance, a Ford chassis outfitted with firefighting gear by Sutphen would be referred to as a Ford/Sutphen.

However "large" apparatus are no longer associated solely with large cities. In rural areas huge tankers and pumper/tankers are used, running on multiple rear axles or semi trailers. Some volunteer departments also operate apparatus that is physically large. This is for at least two reasons. First, compared with large city departments, vol-unteer departments often have a larger number of fire-fighters accompanying each rig; hence they can use more equipment. Second, town and village councils, grateful that they are not paying salaries to their volunteer fire-fighters can afford to be generous when it comes to buying them new equipment.

This volume covers the period from about 1951 until the present. Volume One took us to mid-century. Trucks were well developed, as was the firefighting equipment the truck carried. In this volume, we'll see how apparatus became perfected.

We thank all the sources of photographs whom, we hope, are accurately covered in the credit lines. The late Martha Cedar of White Trucks was the generous source of all the photos credited Volvo/White. We appreciate the help of Ernest N. Day, of New Jersey Fire Equipment Corp., Dick Adelman, Bill Hattersley, Ann-Marie Lamb, Chuck Rhoads, Dick Schneider, Ray Stevens, and Tamara Wood.

Several persons support a fund at San Francisco State University that supports old truck research. We acknowl-edge some of the donors: Stuart B. Abraham, Edward C. Couderc of Sausalito Moving & Storage, Gilbert Hall, Dav-id Kiely, ROADSHOW, Gene Olson, Oshkosh Truck Foun-dation, Charlie Wacker, and Bill West.

Wayne Sorensen
San Jose State University

Donald F. Wood
San Francisco State University
October 1996

Introduction

*A*t the beginning of the 20th century, fire apparatus was horse-drawn. There were many fire stations because horses could run at top speed for only about one-half mile. Fires were reported by using electric alarm boxes that were at major street corners and inside prominent build-ings.

Motorized apparatus was introduced in about 1905 and the period from then until about 1920 witnessed the replacement of the horse. An evolutionary design step was using the truck's engine to both propel the vehicle and power the truck's pump or aerial ladder.

The decade of the 1920s was probably the most explo-sive in terms of spreading the auto culture throughout the United States. The improvements in quality and de-pendability of trucks was reflected in the fire apparatus field. Many of the fire engines and trucks built during the 1920s served in first-line assignments through World War II.

During the 1930s, motor trucks evolved to the point where they could be considered "modern." Relatively few improvements remained to be made. Hydraulics had re-placed mechanics in truck brakes (and in devices for rais-ing aerial ladders).

The 1940s consisted of two halves, when one thinks of fire apparatus. During World War II, large numbers of 1940-style rigs were produced for military and civilian defense needs. Immediately after the war, these same styles were sold to cities that were replacing apparatus that was overdue for retirement. In 1947, American-LaFrance—which had been building some cab-forward apparatus since the late-1930s—introduced its cab-for-ward 700 Series. This model was very popular. These top-ics were covered in Volume One of this series.

The popularity of the American-LaFrance cab-forward design would eventually be adopted by all builders. What other changes will we see in the second half-century's apparatus?

1. The truck chassis will get physically bigger. Existing fire houses often proved to be too small. In any muster when a fire engine from today is parked next to one that is 50 years older, the difference in size is apparent. As for actual truck equipment, today's truck is likely to have automatic transmission, better brakes, and be powered by a diesel engine. One of the longtime distinctions between "custom" apparatus and those mounted on commercial chassis had been that the custom apparatus had dual ignition systems with two spark plugs per cylinder. With the advent of diesels, this distinction was lost.

2. The cab-forward design is almost universal. In addition, firefighters (now of both sexes) no longer cling to the sides and rear of the apparatus as it speeds to the fire. Instead, they are seated inside a cab, often enclosed and air-conditioned. The cab's seats are large and sometimes have hollowed-out rear cushions to accommodate the firefighters' air tanks, which they now use when entering a burning structure.

3. Pumpers are little changed except that they are now usually rated at 1,500 gpm, about twice the capacity of 50 years ago. Fog equipment became popular after World War II. So did a dry chemical system that relied on sodium carbonate, similar to baking soda but treated so it would not cake because of absorbed moisture. Some pumpers are now equipped with rear-mount aerial devices. (In 1985, 15 of Miami's 38 engine companies were equipped with 50-foot Tele-Squrt devices.[1])

4. Ladder trucks show more changes. Some ladders are mounted at the rear of a straight-frame truck, although tractor-drawn aerials remain popular. Some aerials have platforms on top. Snorkels have two arms attached to an elbow and can be placed in more positions than a conventional straight ladder. Aerial ladders are also constructed with lightweight metals, as are some ground ladders. Ground ladders made of wood are preferred when there are overhead streetcar (light rail vehicle) wires. Glued-laminated woods were found to be stronger than those made of solid beams.

5. Two new styles of apparatus are "command posts" and hazardous-materials response units. Command posts are bus-like vehicles with massive communications capability. They are used at major fires or other disaster sites to coordinate and direct many people and pieces of equipment. Hazardous materials incident trucks respond to spills, and both contain the danger and remove the hazardous materials so that they can be properly disposed of. There are also now many airport/aircraft crash trucks. They came into widespread use after World War II.

6. Many departments also operate vehicles that can respond to medical emergencies, and are manned by paramedics. Many firefighters are trained to deal with medical emergencies and most apparatus carry paramedic equipment.

7. Some departments abandoned traditional red in favor of colors more visible at night. Today, one sees many pieces of apparatus that are either painted a light color, or if still red there will be a light colored, often reflectorized, stripe on both sides. However, it appears that "fire engine red" is regaining its popularity.

8. All apparatus carry radios and some carry onboard computers that have information on structures or hazardous materials. Some also carry sophisticated devices for finding their exact location (and making their exact location known to others) via earth satellites. Firefighters carry radios allowing communication with others at the fire scene.

9. Firefighters working inside structures now wear air masks. Apparatus will also carry spare air tanks and some will even carry equipment for recharging the tanks at the fire site.

Two types of equipment that will be eliminated during this new era are water towers and city service (ladder) trucks. Aerial ladder and aerial platform trucks now perform their function.

In paid departments, firefighters' hours of being on-duty were continually reduced and smaller crews were assigned to each company. This meant that, when possible, equipment on apparatus was designed to be operated by fewer firefighters.

In this second half-century we will see nearly all of the major manufacturers of apparatus go out of business. Of the major firms covered in Volume One, only Seagrave remains, located now in Clintonville, Wisconsin, as part of FWD. FWD, itself a supplier of pumpers and ladder trucks during the first half-century, continues to supply chassis for several outfitters whose customers want a fire truck with all-wheel drive capability. Mack continues to build trucks, but no longer builds its own line of firefighting apparatus. They do supply chassis for others to complete.

The number of suppliers of commercial chassis has also decreased since 1950. Brockway, Corbitt, Diamond T, Federal, Reo, and Studebaker dropped out, and Dodge stopped building large chassis in the 1970s. Duplex, Freightliner, and Spartan were three manufacturers whose chassis are often selected by apparatus builders during the second half-century. Sometimes their names are given as the "make" of the truck carrying the apparatus. In other instances, the apparatus builder uses its name for the entire rig. In the commercial motor truck industry, a number of makes, built in either Europe or Japan have sold well in U.S. markets, although few have ended up in the U.S. fire service.

Perusing both volumes of this set will show how this nation's fire apparatus has evolved from horse-drawn rigs at the beginning of the century.

---

[1]   Firehouse (September, 1985), p. 141.

Chapter 1
1951-1960

At the war's end, cities began re-equipping their departments, making up for a five-year lapse during which it was nearly impossible to acquire new apparatus unless needed to protect war production facilities. An article about Philadelphia read:

> Before the war it was known the rehabilitation was needed and over $300,000 was made available. Then all at once nothing could be purchased. Came 1946 and an adverse report by engineers of the National Board of Fire Underwriters. The $750,000 was spent for 32 Autocar 750-gallon pumping engines, 24 Ford/Hale booster combinations, six American-LaFrance 85-foot aerial trucks, four Peter Pirsch 85-foot aerials, seven Fords for battalion chiefs, a rescue truck on International chassis, and the $175,000 *Bernard Samuel*, first of three new diesel fireboats.[1]

The new diesel fireboats replaced fireboats that burned either coal or oil continuously to maintain steam for power. The diesel fireboat's engine was run only when needed. Philadelphia also established an Emergency Crew and equipped it with a war-surplus army wrecker, a floodlight wagon, a refueling tanker, a lubricating truck, and some panel body trucks. The crew performed some equipment maintenance and also served at fires, responding to extra alarms or special calls.

Turning to a medium-size city, Hammond, Indiana, here's a roster of its equipment in 1951, kept at six firehouses:

- Station One had a 1942 Mack Squad truck, a 1926 American-LaFrance pumper, a 1949 American-LaFrance 100-foot aerial, and a 1948 International carbon dioxide truck.

- Station Two housed a 1947 Mack pumper and also housed two reserve rigs: a 1930 American-LaFrance 85-foot aerial and a 1925 Ahrens-Fox pumper.

- Station Three kept a 1930 Seagrave pumper, a 1942 DeSoto ambulance, and a 1948 Ford service truck.

- Station Four was home to a 1930 Seagrave pumper and a 1930 American-LaFrance ladder truck.

- Station Five housed a 1930 Seagrave pumper.

- Station Six had a 1947 Mack pumper.

Hammond was expecting to receive two new pumpers, a ladder truck, and an ambulance. They employed 58 firemen classified as "privates" who were paid $3,600 annually, plus a $100 clothing allowance. There were also 22 drivers, 10 lieutenants, 10 captains, 2 assistant chiefs and a chief. The department relied on telephones and a Gamewell alarm system for receiving reports of fires.[2]

The fire department is but one element of a community's overall efforts at preventing and suppressing fires. An article appearing in 1954 showed the weights that the National Board of Fire Underwriters gave to various factors. They were: water supply, 34 percent; fire department, 30 percent; fire alarm system, 11 percent; building laws, 4 percent; fire prevention, 6 percent;

[1] *The American City* (April 1951), p 129.

[2] *The American City* (June 1951), p. 95.

and structural conditions, 14 percent.[3] Training of firefighters would become more important during this second half-century. Physical fitness was important and many departments expected their men to keep in shape with regular exercise. In 1953, in Miami, it was said that "every fireman must play at least one game of volleyball each day. . . ."[4]

The National Board of Fire Underwriters had considerable influence on equipment design. For example, in 1956, it required all pumpers be rated while producing 150 psi; and that the minimum sizes of booster tanks be 200 gallons.[5] In essence, this meant that municipalities would write these values into their specifications as they asked for bids from manufacturers for new equipment.

In Oak Park, Michigan, the duties of police and firemen were combined with most of them on police patrol and the fire stations were manned only by drivers who would respond to alarms and be met at the fire site by others arriving in police patrol cars. Frequently the police cars would arrive at the fire first, so they were all equipped with light firefighting equipment. Several other communities—such as Evanston, Illinois—tried this approach, although it was never widely adopted. In 1960, the National Board of Fire Underwriters, when looking at such systems, would rate the policeman/fireman riding in a police car as one-fourth the equivalent of a firefighter who rode with the fire engine. Experience in Evanston was that in 44 fires the policemen/firemen arrived before the engine, in 68 cases they arrived at the same time, in 44 cases they arrived within two minutes of the engine, and in 24 cases it was more than two minutes after the engine.[6] Dearborn equipped its police station wagons with five-pound carbon dioxide extinguishers and, in 1960, the policemen extinguished 22 fires before the fire engines arrived. Sunnyvale, California, also combined the duties of police and firemen.

This was also the era of the Cold War and there was fear of nuclear attack. Fire chiefs and their departments became a part of a "Civil Defense" network, designed to deal with the aftermath of a nuclear attack. Luckily, the nuclear attack never came but some of the regional coordinating devices that were established proved useful for dealing with natural disasters. Civil Defense funds also became available for equipment purchase. In Boston, a special division of the fire department worked on Civil Defense matters and had "long-range plans to coordinate the action of the fire department during an enemy attack with the overall functioning of Civil Defense in the metropolitan area. Air-raid tests have been held, and many of Boston's fire houses are equipped with huge air-raid sirens that echo weirdly across the rooftops during a practice alert."[7] In 1953, Kansas City, Missouri, purchased three air-raid sirens, each powered by a 180-hp Chrysler engine, which were placed on the city hall, and two other buildings. The remainder of the city was "served by smaller motor-driven sirens located on school buildings and fire stations. Where dead spots can be determined, smaller sirens will be mounted."[8]

Civil defense measures required additional training. For example, in the District of Columbia, all fire companies practiced drawing water from the Potomac and Anacostia Rivers, which skirt Washington, D.C.

> One or more pumpers are placed at the edge of the river, with suction pipes dropped in. A set of two lines of hose (two lines instead of one reduces the loss of pressure by friction) is run from each pumper to a second pumper as far as 4,000 feet. . . . The only limiting factor to the distance water can be relayed is the number of pumpers available and the footage of hose at hand. . . . Every source of water in the Washington area has been located and listed on charts of the city and suburbs. These include creeks, ponds, reservoirs, and even swimming pools.[9]

The water main system in U.S. cities was always considered vulnerable to bombing. San Francisco, with its history of earthquakes, had a number of cisterns filled with water located a major intersections from which a pumper could draw water. San Francisco and other major cities also had "high pressure" hydrant systems, usually serving industrial or high-fire-risk areas with ex-

[3] *The American City* (October 1954), p. 5.

[4] *The American City* (May 1953), p. 129.

[5] *The American City* (December 1956), p. 55.

[6] *The American City* (September 1960), p. 176.

[7] *The American City* (August 1952), p. 84.

[8] *The American City* (June 1953), p. 18.

[9] *The American City* (November 1951), p. 117.

tra-large diameter mains that fed hydrants, independent of the regular municipal water supply. In 1952, it was reported that:

> Boston has a high-pressure system of water supply consisting of 19 miles of mains 12, 16, and 20 inches in diameter, with 506 hydrants of 2,000 gallons capacity each, spaced about 150 feet apart. This is grid-ironed throughout one square mile of the high-value district, providing a water supply (independent of the municipal supply) for firefighting only. This system eliminates the use of a large number of fire engines and thus simplifies operations.[10]

During the 1950s, FDNY (Fire Department of New York) received an order of 30 Ward LaFrance pumpers to meet requirements of the area's "Atomic Bomb Plan." FDNY added many interesting specialized apparatus during the decade. In 1951, they placed into service a mobile lubrication unit that would travel from station to station performing routine services to each piece of apparatus. By 1952, all FDNY apparatus had two-way radios. Two step van communications posts were added in 1953. In 1955, FDNY received what would be its last new wooden aerial ladders. In 1957, a van was equipped to recharge oxygen masks and tanks at fire sites, or at stations. An old canteen truck was modified to carry radiological testing devices.

Private salvage corps continued to be absorbed by municipal departments. In Baltimore, the Corps bought a 1953 White to replace a unit destroyed in a collision with a pumper en route to a fire.

In our *American Volunteer Fire Trucks* book and in Volume One of this set, considerable discussion was devoted to "shop-built" apparatus, i.e. apparatus built in fire department shops using labor provided by firefighters. In small towns this work might be done by volunteers working in a blacksmith shop or garage. In the second half of the century fewer examples can be found of shop-built rigs. However, a few examples do appear in this book. An item in the October 1954 issue of *The American City* said that Sapulpa, Oklahoma, used a Chevrolet cab-over-engine chassis to build a rig to fight brush fires. It carried an American-LaFrance pump, which local firemen installed, plus a 410-gallon tank. It was used to save "wear and tear" on that city's first class American-LaFrance pumper and aerial ladder. Indianapolis and San Jose shops turned out some apparatus in

the 1950s. In the same decade, Houston's shops built an airport crash truck that carried foam equipment, and a light truck that carried 16 floodlights.

One new style of apparatus to develop was the elevating platform, soon known as "snorkel." Chicago's fire commissioner, Robert J. Quinn, is credited with the idea, which he reportedly got while observing sign repairmen using a "boom and bucket" device. Pitman Manufacturing Co., of Grandview, Missouri, supplied the device, which was placed on a 1958 GMC chassis. A monitor and 3-1/2-inch hose were attached. The boom carrying the platform had an elbow, giving the snorkel the ability to move in many more directions than could a conventional aerial ladder. Chicago's original snorkel had a 50-foot boom. By 1960, Chicago had three more snorkels in service, with the latter three towers supplied by Mobile Aerial Towers, Inc., of Indianapolis. The snorkels carried the trade name of "Hi-Ranger" and had booms of 65 feet, 75 feet, and 85 feet, respectively. Within only a few years, the device achieved great popularity. By 1960, elevating platforms were being installed by a number of apparatus builders and outfitters including American-LaFrance, Crown, Pierce, Van Pelt, and Ward LaFrance.

The new style of warning light that came into use looked like a gumball-dispensing machine and was mounted at the top of the truck's windshield or roof. One or more bulbs rotated inside. The rotating beacon was similar to that in a lighthouse. Its main advantage was that it was visible from all sides. A few cities had the ability to control traffic signals on main streets. The officer in the lead fire apparatus responding to a fire would radio headquarters as they moved along and have headquarters adjust street lights to allow the fire apparatus to drive through.

A 1959 survey determined numbers of apparatus, by state, that were in communities of 10,000 or more people. The numbers were: Alabama, 129; Alaska, 5; Arizona, 33; Arkansas, 61; California, 897; Colorado, 67; Connecticut, 291; Delaware, 21; District of Columbia, 81; Florida, 188; Georgia, 147; Idaho, 32; Illinois, 480; Indiana, 256; Iowa, 164; Kansas, 103; Kentucky, 62; Louisiana, 152; Maine, 76; Maryland, 103; Massachusetts, 656; Michigan, 373; Minnesota, 152; Mississippi, 64; Missouri, 195; Montana, 44; Nebraska, 62; Nevada, 17; New Hampshire, 60; New Jersey, 461; New Mexico, 41; New York, 872; North Carolina, 184; North Dakota, 31; Ohio,

---

[10] *The American City* (August 1952), pp. 83-84.

491; Oklahoma, 156; Oregon, 92; Pennsylvania, 526; Rhode Island, 106; South Carolina, 72; South Dakota, 33; Tennessee, 125; Texas, 603; Utah, 38; Vermont, 15; Virginia, 204; Washington, 153; West Virginia, 78; Wisconsin, 217; and Wyoming, 21.[11]

After World War II most growth in urban areas was in the surrounding suburbs. Often these would be in a different jurisdiction than the central city's fire department. Suburbs were less densely developed and had wide streets and few tall buildings. The area protected by each station was large, in geographic terms, and relatively few ladder trucks were needed. The telephone became the common way to report a fire. (In Houston, in 1953, 2,510 alarms were received from its Gamewell box system and 4,289 by telephone.[12]) Soon the old alarm systems relying on corner call-boxes would be gradually dismantled, although in some cities there was considerable controversy as to whether they should be eliminated. In big cities, false alarms sent in via alarm boxes were to become an increasing problem.

Stations built in the suburbs were usually single-story with the sleeping and living quarters on the ground floor, adjacent to the apparatus room. Fire stations built in the mid-1950s in Birmingham, Michigan, incorporated a new idea that apparently never caught on. That idea was to substitute stainless steel slides for the traditional fireman's brass pole.[13]

One new form of development common to many new suburbs was the shopping mall. Departments responsible for their protection had to be concerned with access to the buildings, use of sprinkler systems, etc. Some shopping centers were built in areas with few or no building codes.

In the mid-1950s, West Milwaukee, a suburb of Milwaukee, formed its own fire department. Formerly it had contracted with the City of Milwaukee to perform its fire protection services, but the City of Milwaukee raised its fees to the point where West Milwaukee decided to equip and man a department of its own. They purchased a ladder truck and three pumpers, all Seagraves. Relationships between cities and suburbs involved many factors, and often there was political conflict. In Los Angeles County, in 1959, the County Fire Department provided fire protection for 1.2 million residents in the county's unincorporated areas. As new communities incorporated, they often contracted with the county for fire protection service and the County Fire Department would often man a station in the community's downtown. Some older communities also turned to the county department to meet their needs. In mid-1959, the County Department provided first call response for 18 cities and had mutual aid agreements with 32 other cities. At that time the entire mutual aid program was being revamped because of new Civil Defense programs.

When major cities annexed suburbs they often assumed responsibilities for protecting some rural and otherwise undeveloped areas. Dispatching became difficult for departments with responsibilities covering wide geographic areas. For a time, the dispatchers for Baltimore County used microfilm maps showing all of the sites, alarm boxes, hydrants, and road networks. Maps were filed by street intersections.

The Los Angeles Police Department began using a helicopter for traffic enforcement and, during the unit's first year of service, it reported 37 fires via radio. In one instance it warned residents of a grass fire by flying low, causing people to step outside and become aware of the smoke and spreading fire.

In the mid-1950s, Ahrens-Fox introduced its cab-forward design (built by C.D. Beck), but sales were slow and soon the firm ceased production of new apparatus. Ahrens-Fox had been best-known for its pumpers with the distinctive polished globe in front. Its old engines are highly prized by museums and collectors.

American Fire Apparatus of Battle Creek, Michigan, made deliveries, mainly to smaller departments.

The 1950s were "glory days" for American-LaFrance, which was considered the industry's leader. Its popular 700 series, powered by V-12 engines, was in great demand. Competitors would copy the cab-forward design. Keeping ahead of the competition, American-LaFrance introduced its 800 series in 1956, and its 900 series in 1958. The 900 series had a wrap-around windshield, dual headlights, and eight possible powerplants.

Coast, of Martinez, California, built apparatus sold mainly in northern California. It used International, and some Peterbilt chassis.

[11] Automobile Manufacturers Association, *1960 Motor Truck Facts* (Detroit, 1960), page 44. Figures were not given for Hawaii.

[12] *The American City* (October 1954), p. 92.

[13] *The American City* (March 1956), p. 23.

Crown, a longtime Los Angeles truck body and school bus body builder, introduced its open cab-forward Fire Coach in about 1950. Sales were to be mainly in Southern California, Arizona, and Hawaii. Crown apparatus is frequently seen in movies and television shows filmed in the Los Angeles area. Custom Crown apparatus tended to be expensive, but it sold well. Quoted delivery times sometimes averaged 450 days. Only one standard pumper was available on a 175-inch chassis, although it could be equipped in many different ways.

Duplex had been an obscure truck building firm in Lansing, Michigan, since before World War I. In 1953, Howe began buying Duplex chassis for mounting its bodies. In this same decade, Duplex also supplied its chassis to Zabek Fire Apparatus, of Palmer, Massachusetts, which also built apparatus on them. In 1955, Duplex became part of Warner and Swasey Co., and soon would become an important supplier of chassis to a number of custom apparatus builders.

Ford was neither an apparatus builder nor outfitter, but mention should be made of one of its commercial chassis models since it was to become important to the fire service. Introduced in 1957, the Ford C-series was a cab-forward model with a flat front and compact Budd-built cab that tilted forward, giving access to the engine. In terms of longevity, the Ford C would surpass even the Mack Bulldog. Ford Cs are common to the fire service and no doubt outsell other makes of commercial chassis used for carrying apparatus.

FWD continued in the apparatus business supplying a few large orders to big cities, as well as individual sales to small communities that wanted the truck's superior traction. FWD also supplied some chassis to Pierce. In the late 1950s, FWD signed an agreement with Geesink, an aerial ladder builder located in the Netherlands, for rights to sell its rear-mount aerials in the United States. In 1959, the firm introduced its cab-forward fire apparatus chassis.

The George Heiser Body Co. of Seattle, a firm still in existence, outfitted many chassis, usually Kenworths, for cities in the Pacific Northwest. It also worked with L.N. Curtis Co., of Oakland, which was the West Coast distributor for Maxim apparatus and Hale pumps.

Howard-Cooper, of Portland, Oregon, ceased building fire apparatus. The firm continues to this day selling logging, mining, and construction equipment.

General of St. Louis ceased building apparatus in 1956, although it continued to manufacture fire extinguishers.

In 1953, Richmond, California, bought one of the first "command" vehicles, with an International Metro (step van) body. It carried six different radio sets, necessary to communicate with various other emergency agencies in the area, and had a roof-mounted speaker for its public address system. In keeping with the Civil Defense worries of that era, it also carried equipment for monitoring radiation.

In early 1951, Little Rock, Arkansas, took delivery of a Jeep rescue wagon that carried a 14-foot boat on a roof rack and a 10-hp Johnson outboard motor. It also carried a portable generator, tools, and a resuscitator. Some cities purchased Jeeps for fighting brush fires and they were popular with small town departments and forestry agencies.

In 1959, Larry Leicher left International Harvester and returned to the Luverne Fire Apparatus Co. of Luverne, Minnesota, to take charge of production. He was a son of one of the brothers who founded the firm.

Mack produced and sold many fire apparatus during this period. About 1950, the firm introduced a new 75-foot aerial and, in 1955, a tractor-drawn aerial (with the ladder supplied by Maxim). The Mack C-series was designed for fire apparatus only and had been acquired from Ahrens-Fox and its successor Beck in 1956. It was a cab-forward design, which was of growing popularity. In 1959, Mack delivered two Magirus 146-foot rear-mount aerial ladders to Chicago.

In 1952, Maxim acquired the North American license for the German-built Magirus aerial ladder. The mounted ladder required a chassis only slightly longer than that of a conventional Maxim pumper. Maxim introduced its own cab-forward models in 1959. Most Maxim apparatus of this era used Hale pumps, although other builders often relied on Maxim to supply aerial ladders.

Oren-Roanoke Corp., of Roanoke, Virginia, produced Oren apparatus. It relied on commercial chassis, including Corbitt. The firm utilized Duplex chassis for its custom rigs.

In 1960, the Auto Body Works of Appleton, Wisconsin, changed its name to Pierce Auto Body Works. It was becoming increasingly involved in the production of fire apparatus, having recently delivered 40 Civil Defense trailers outfitted with Darley pumps to Minneapolis. It was also working with the Pitman Co. to develop a body for that company's articulating boom.

Pirsch's sales were good after World War II. It had an especially fine reputation as a builder of aerial ladder trucks. Sales during this decade went to large cities including: Atlanta, Chicago,

Los Angeles, Memphis, Minneapolis, New York City, and Salt Lake City.

Seagrave introduced a new design in 1951 and called it its "70th Anniversary" model. It was more streamlined than the previous model with headlights mounted in the fenders and a siren in a circle just under the top of the hood. It looked streamlined, but in a bulky sort of way. Also the engine was in front of the cab at the time the industry was moving to cab-forward designs. Seagrave, itself, introduced its cab-forward design in 1959. For readers interested in "quads" and "quints," mention should be made of a 1956 quad that Seagrave delivered to Hamtramck, Michigan. It was a trailer-drawn aerial with a 1,000-gpm pump mounted on the tractor. It carried no hose (except for suction hose) so it qualifies only as a "quad" rather than a "quint." It was not popular because pumping required being near a hydrant, which might not be where the aerial ladder was needed. It's pictured in Walt McCall's *American Fire Engines Since 1900* with the observa-tion "This is certainly one of the most unusual quadruple combinations ever built."[14]

Van Pelt was located in Oakdale, California, and initially had supplied tankers to rural fire departments in northern California. It began supplying equipment for large cities, often relying on Diamond T and Kenworth chassis, Hall-Scott engines, and Hale pumps. In 1960, Van Pelt built its first custom rig, and delivered it to Mountain View, California.

Ward LaFrance continued to be a major supplier of apparatus for FDNY. Many of its sales to FDNY during the 1950s were for "Civil Defense" pumpers, paid for with federal funds in an effort to help prepare the nation's major cities for the possibilities of an atomic bomb drop. "CD" emblems can be seen on many apparatus of this era. Civil Defense plans also set up many of the regional disaster agencies that are in operation today.

Westates, a California firm founded in 1956, slowly grew into a major regional supplier. It relied on commercial chassis and Waterous pumps.

---

[14] p. 278.

An American-LaFrance Type 0-10 U.S. Air Force crash truck. The unit carried fire fighting chemical agents. It's shown being loaded on an Air Force troop and cargo carrier. (Photo courtesy Wayne Sorensen)

An early 1950s American-LaFrance crash truck used at Detroit's airport. It looks like it has all-wheel drive.

Clyde, New York, ran this quad built on a 1951 Diamond T chassis by Young Fire Equipment Co., of Buffalo. (Photo courtesy Young Fire Equipment Co.)

The San Jose, California, Fire Department built this unusual light, foam, and salvage unit on a 1951 Ford chassis. The unit carries 120 gallons of foam, and is equipped with a five-kw light unit developing 5,000 watts. (Photo courtesy Wayne Sorensen)

The Seattle Fire Department converted this 1951 GMC Army surplus 6x6 into a foam unit. The unit carries five-gallon foam containers, high expansion foam containers and a high expansion foam generator. The foam truck was a special call apparatus only. (Photo courtesy Bill Hattersley)

Coast used this 1951 International Model R-306 chassis to build Oakland, California's Engine 8. The pumper has a 1,250-gpm Waterous pump, and a 150-gallon booster tank. It was powered by a 480 Hall-Scott six-cylinder, 275-hp engine. (Photo courtesy Wayne Sorensen)

1951 International Model R-306 open cab chassis used by Coast to build Oakland, California's Engine 17. The pumper is equipped with a 1,250-gpm Waterous pump and a mounted turret and water tank. (Photo courtesy Wayne Sorensen)

A 1951 Kenworth pumper by Van Pelt with a 1,000-gpm Hale pump and a 400-gallon booster tank. Note the pre-connected hard suction hose wrapped around the front of the engine compartment. In service as Engine 8 in Sacramento. (Photo courtesy Wayne Sorensen)

Van Pelt was a prominent apparatus builder for cities on the West Coast. Kenworth was a popular chassis for use in the West. Engine 3 of Stockton, California, ran a 1951 Kenworth-Van Pelt with a 1,250-gpm Hale pump and 500-gallon water tank. Photo shows an excellent view of wrap-around squirrel tail pre-connected hard suction. (Photo courtesy Paccar)

Two 1951 Mack Type 95 chassis were purchased new by the San Francisco Fire Department. Turret and hose bodies were not installed until 1955 due to the lack of funds. Then a Gorter turret and hose body were built and installed by fire department shops. Hose Tender 15 placed back in-service at the time of 1989 earthquake. Rig now is heavily laden with 4,000 feet of five-inch hose, three portable hydrants and five Gleeson valves. Photo taken in 1991, with Bay Bridge in background. (Photo courtesy Photo Wayne Sorensen)

American-LaFrance cab-forward apparatus was very popular. This 750-gpm pumper ran in Dillon, South Carolina. (Photo courtesy Dick Adelman)

This 1952 Autocar served as an auxiliary piece of fire apparatus because it was equipped with a water tank and pump. Its primary duties were washing the roadways, ceilings and walls inside the tunnels operated by the Port of New York Tunnel Authority. Note sweeps in front and the array of nozzles in the rear. The separate pumping unit consisted of a 500-gpm Champion pump powered by a Chrysler engine. The builder was H & H Truck Tank, Inc., of Jersey City. The versatile truck also had a snow plow mounting in the front. (Photo courtesy Watson & Meehan)

Fresno's Fire Department shops built this city service truck on a 1952 GMC chassis. (Photo courtesy Wayne Sorensen)

Military fire apparatus was disposed of as surplus and often ended up in small communities. This 1952 Howe-Defender, with a 750-gpm pump, found a second life in Rabbit Creek, Alaska. (Photo courtesy Wayne Sorensen)

Military bases required fire protection and both military and civilian crews were used. This early 1950s International was outfitted as a 500-gpm pumper by Darley, to protect the Coast Guard Reserve Training Center at Yorktown. (Photo courtesy Darley)

The "A" series Mack saw considerable service in fire departments. Shown is Buffalo's 1952 750-gpm airport crash truck with a mounted turret, and tandem rear axles to carry weight of water. Note the sweeps below bumper. (Photo courtesy Dick Adelman)

A 1952 Pirsch 750-gpm canopy cab pumper used by Ocean City, New Jersey as Engine 4. "Gumball"-type of rotating light, as seen on top of cab, became popular during the 1950s. Their advantage was that they could be seen from all directions. (Photo courtesy Ernest N. Day)

Charlotte, North Carolina, ran this 1953 American-LaFrance with a 1,000-gpm pump. Note pump panel is on truck's right side. Also visible on this side of cab is a radio antenna. (Photo courtesy John J. Robrecht & Dick Adelman)

Bodywork on this 1953 Autocar was by U.S. Fire Apparatus Co. of Wilmington. The vehicle has a 750-gpm Hale two-stage centrifugal pump and 250-gallon booster tank, and was used by the Gladwyne Fire Department in Pennsylvania's Montgomery County. (Photo courtesy Volvo/White)

This 1953 Autocar 750-gpm pumper with a 650-gallon booster tank was built by U.S. Fire Apparatus Co. for use in Lakewood, New York. The unit has a sleeper cab converted to seat eight firefighters. The booster reels are mounted above the pump. The pump was a Barton-American. (Photo courtesy Volvo/White)

A 1953 Diamond T used as Rescue Squad 3 in Chicago. (Photo courtesy American Trucking Associations)

The Chicago Fire Department placed an order for 30 FWD pumpers in 1953. Shown is Engine 53 a Model F-1000-T FWD equipped with a Waterous 1,000-gpm two-stage centrifugal pump and all-wheel drive, and powered by a Wauke-sha six-cylinder, 240-hp engine. (Photo courtesy Bob Freeman & Dick Adelman)

A 1953 Kenworth Model 721 chassis was used by Van-Pelt for Engine 31 of Oakland, California. This pumper had an open cab, a Hale two-stage, 1,000-gpm centrifugal pump, 290-gallon booster tank with a 100-gpm booster pump. (Photo courtesy Wayne Sorensen)

A 1953 Peterbilt pumper built by Coast for Dinuba, California. The 1,000-gpm pumper has an extra-long hard suction hose pre-connected to a swivel for quick hookup. The power is a 169 Hall-Scott engine. (Photo courtesy Coast)

Three Pirsch 1,000-gpm pumpers were purchased in 1953 by the Chicago Fire Department. Notice the bell cut-out in the grille. Engine 43 has an International cab and was powered by a Waukesha engine. (Photo courtesy Bob Freeman & Dick Adelman)

A circa-1953 Seagrave tractor-drawn 100-foot aerial. It has been equipped with a shop-built cab for riot protection, and the tiller seat cab has also been protected. It was Washington, D.C.'s Truck 10. The white band around the middle of the red tractor was for improved visibility. (Photo courtesy Dick Adelman)

Hot Springs, Arkansas, operated this 1954 American-LaFrance that carried a 750-gpm pump. An Ansul chemical extinguisher was carried in front corner nearest the camera. A short FM radio antenna is barely visible above cab. (Photo courtesy Dick Adelman)

A 1954 American-LaFrance 0-11 crash truck, used by the U.S. Air Force at Gowen Field, near Boise, Idaho. (Photo courtesy Wayne Sorensen)

Chicago received eight cab-over-engine Autocar Squad Trucks in 1954. They were equipped with large four-door cabs and had equipment compartments on each side of the box. The units carried a four-way turret mounted behind the cab. Shown is Flying Squad 6. (Photo courtesy Dick Adelman)

A 1954 Duplex-Zabec 750-gpm pumper with a 380-gallon booster tank. In service as Atlantic City's Engine 3. (Photo courtesy John J. Robrecht & Dick Adelman)

St. Louis operated this rescue squad mounted on a 1954 International chassis. "CD" stands for Civil Defense, meaning that truck was also under nominal control of the Civil Defense agency in case of a major emergency. (Photo courtesy Robert Pauly)

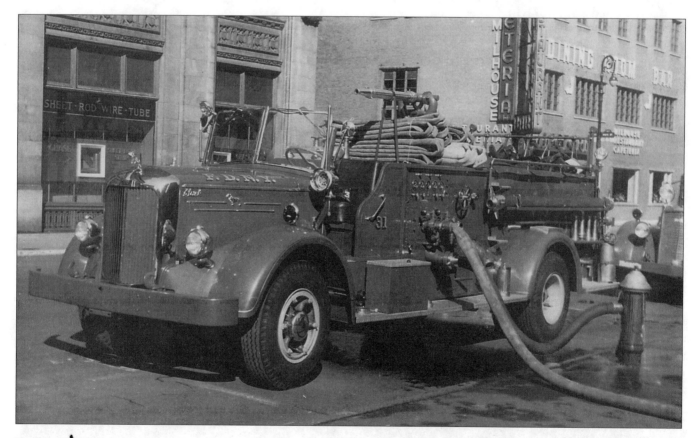

Twenty-five Mack pumpers were delivered to New York City in 1954. Shown is FDNY Engine 31. These pumpers had high-pressure, four-stage 1,000-gpm pumps with a mounted turret. Cab has no doors. (Photo courtesy Charles E. Beckwith)

Philadelphia, Pennsylvania's Ladder 1's 1954-Maxim-Magirus 100-foot rear-turntable aerial. This truck did not carry a full complement of ground ladders because the ground ladders had to be removed to use the turntable. (Photo courtesy John J. Robrecht & Dick Adelman)

Nashville used this 1954 custom Oren 750-gpm triple combination. It was Engine 17.

Sacramento's rescue squad built on a 1954 Peterbilt chassis with bodywork by Coast. The squad had a 1,000-gpm Waterous pump and a 400-gallon water tank. The power was a Model 855 Hall-Scott 265-hp engine. The rescue squad truck was later painted red and ran as Engine 7. (Photo courtesy Wayne Sorensen)

A 1954 Peterbilt-Coast with a 1,250-gpm Waterous pump and a 400-gallon booster tank, initially built as a rescue squad and painted white. Shown here, it is a reserve engine painted red in 1976. The powerplant was a 855 Hall-Scott, six-cylinder, 265-hp engine. (Photo courtesy Wayne Sorensen).

In 1954, Coast used a Peterbilt closed cab chassis to build a large 1,000-gpm pumper for Engine 5, at Grants Pass, Oregon.

A 1955 Coast Custom Chassis Quadruple, short wheelbase unit on an International chassis, built for Oakland, California, to run as Engine 24. This engine was equipped with a 1,250-gpm, two-stage centrifugal pump, and a 250-gallon booster tank. The power was a 935 G-1 Hall-Scott six-cylinder, 294-hp engine. All ladders are metal. (Photo courtesy Wayne Sorensen)

In 1955, New York City purchased 25 wood 75-foot aerials from the FWD Corporation. Tops over crew seat and over tiller seat built later to protect firemen from objects thrown by rioters. Shown is H&L 163. (Photo courtesy Dick Adelman)

Newark, New Jersey's Engine 20 pumping at a large fire. The hood is open to help cool the engine. The pumper is a circa-1955 FWD half cab with a 1,000-gpm pump. (Photo courtesy Dick Adelman)

Bendix, Ohio, bought this 1955 GMC with a Sutphen body. Note hose in tray behind front inlet. Bell is on left. (Photo courtesy Sutphen)

St. Louis purchased two Howe Defender 1,000-gpm triple combination pumpers on Duplex chassis in 1955. The pumpers are equipped with wrap-around pre-connected hard suction hose. Shown is Engine 30. (Photo courtesy Robert Pauly)

Swampscott, Maine, ran this 1955 Maxim that had a 750-gpm pump. The photo was taken at a muster held in Pembroke, New Hampshire. (Photo courtesy Roland Boulet)

Cottage Grove, Maryland's 1955 Seagrave Anniversary Safety Sedan rescue squad with side mounted compartments. Notice the chrome-plated upper radiator shell and white roof and top of hood. (Photo courtesy Dick Adelman)

A 1956 Ahrens-Fox-Beck Model ECB, 750-gpm centrifugal triple combination built for Engine 2 of East Rutherford, New Jersey. Mack acquired this cab forward design when Mack purchased C.D. Beck in the fall of 1956. (Photo courtesy Beck)

Engine 38 in St. Louis was this 1956 American-LaFrance 1,000-gpm pumper. (Photo courtesy Robert Pauly)

St. Louis ran this 1956 American-LaFrance 85-foot aerial on a tractor-trailer. Siren is mounted in nose of the enclosed cab, between headlights. (Photo courtesy Dick Adelman)

Dundas, Ontario, Canada, operated this 1956 American-LaFrance 1,000-gpm pumper. Note overhead ladder rack. (Photo courtesy Dick Adelman)

A 1956 Crown Firecoach, Model CP-100-59, 1,000-gpm triple combination with a 400-gallon booster tank built for Hagginwood, California, which was later annexed by Sacramento. Shown here is Engine 18 of Sacramento. (Photo courtesy Wayne Sorensen)

The New Jersey Fire Equipment Corp. of Dunellen, New Jersey, was a Pirsch dealer, sold Goodrich fire hose, and also outfitted and sold apparatus under the "Great Eastern" name. This Great Eastern custom 750-gpm pump was built on an Oren chassis in 1956. Buyer was Pennsauken, New Jersey. Note "eyebrows" over headlights, a common accessory during the 1950s. (Photo courtesy Ernest N. Day)

Howard-Cooper built some interesting apparatus in its final years. Shown is Asotin, Washington's Engine 2, a 1956 Kenworth 750-gpm triple combination with a 500-gallon tank. (Photo courtesy Bill Hattersley)

A shop-built ladder and 1,250-gpm pump truck on 1956 Peterbilt chassis No. M-1124 for Fresno's Truck 4. Later, it was built into 2,600-gallon tanker No. 3. (Photo courtesy Wayne Sorensen)

Seagrave delivered two 1956, 70th Anniversary Series, Model 900 B, 1,000-gpm combination pumpers to San Francisco. They came with half-cabs and had the Seagrave V-12, 300-hp engines. These combinations were converted to triples in 1961 by the addition of 400-gallon booster tanks by department shops. Shown is Engine 43. (Photo courtesy Wayne Sorensen)

A 1957 International panel delivery with all-wheel drive, used as a Civil Defense rescue unit in Watonga, Oklahoma. (Photo courtesy Office of Civil Defense)

Milwaukee's Ladder 9, a 1957 Mack B Series chassis used by Milwaukee to mount a German-made four-section Magirus 100-foot aerial with four stabilizer jacks. (Photo courtesy Dick Adelman)

San Jose's 1958 American-LaFrance 900 Series with a restyled cab featuring a wrap-around windshield. The power was a V-12 engine, and the rig was a 1,250-gpm triple combination with a 500-gallon booster tank. (Photo courtesy Wayne Sorensen)

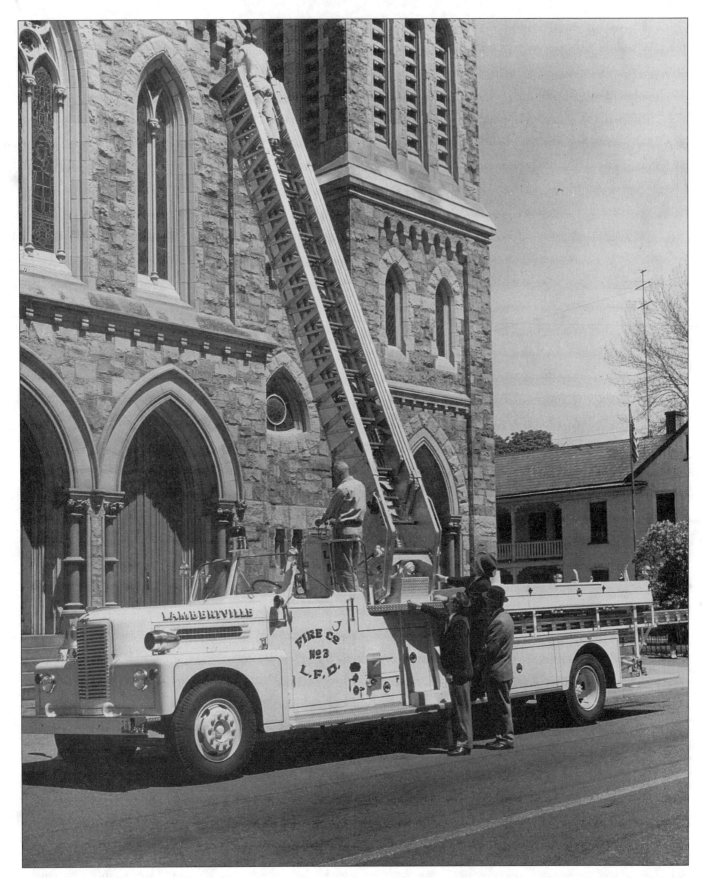

A 1957 Pirsch on a straight frame with a 75-foot aerial being raised in front of a church. Truck was used in Lambertville, New Jersey. It's shown going through its acceptance tests. (Photo courtesy Ernest N. Day)

A 1958 Diamond T COE Model 723C with heavy-duty tilt-cab. This design later sold to International, and Hendrickson also used this cab. The design has a dip in the bottom of the side ventilator wing window. This tractor was outfitted to pull Truck 11's wooden aerial ladder for Elizabeth, New Jersey. (Photo courtesy Mort Glasofer)

A Chicago fire (on New Years Day) 1958. Barely visible at the right are a 1923 Seagrave 65-foot spring raised, hand-cranked water tower, and two 1954 Autocar Squads with turret streams directed on fire; in the right foreground is a Civil Defense Rescue 1954 Reo-Boyertown and two Pirsch 100-foot aerials are at the left of the photo. (Photo courtesy Defense Civil Preparedness Agency-Department of Defense)

Chicago used this 1958 GMC chassis to build its first snorkel. It had a 50-foot Pitman elevating platform. Elevating platforms had been used previously by tree-trimmers and for sign maintenance.

Seattle purchased six 1958 Mack B-Series-Heiser 1,500-gpm pumpers. This Mack has a longer and higher hood to accommodate its Hall-Scott 324-hp gasoline engine. Shown is Engine 38, a triple combination with enclosed cab and 200-gallon booster tank. (Photo courtesy Wayne Sorensen)

A 1958 Mack B Series half-cab 1,250-gpm pumper built for Engine 50 in Boston. A covering has been built over the crew seat and tailboard to protect firemen from thrown objects. (Photo courtesy Dick Adelman)

A 1958 Mack-Magirus 146-foot aerial used by Chicago as Truck 39. Mack called this a Model B85F, the cab and hood are from a discontinued L Series. (Photo courtesy Dick Adelman)

In 1959, the Citrus Heights Fire Protection District north of Sacramento purchased the first diesel pumper sold on the West Coast. It was a Coast Custom Model 1500, powered with a Detroit 8V-71 diesel. The pumper was a semi-cab forward 1,250-gpm triple combination with a 300-gallon water tank. (Photo courtesy Wayne Sorensen)

A 1959 Ford Hi-Ranger 75-foot snorkel, with bodywork by Pierce, serving as Snorkel 2 in Chicago. (Photo courtesy Dan G. Martin)

One of the first Curtis-Heiser pumpers was built on a 1959 Ford C tilt cab chassis for King County Fire District located at Burien, Washington. The pumper had a 1,250-gpm Hale pump and 500-gallon water tank. Notice the low compartments. The Ford "C" chassis, introduced in 1957, was to have the longest production run of any U.S. truck, and was popular in the fire service. (Photo courtesy Bill Hattersley)

A 1959 Ford-High Ranger 85-foot snorkel used by Chicago as Snorkel 4. It is shown out of service at department shops. (Photo courtesy Dick Adelman)

Ann Arbor, Michigan, used this circa-1959 International COE city service truck. This cab style was purchased from Diamond T. Note the siren mounted in the grille. (Photo courtesy National Automotive History Collection, Detroit Public Library)

New York City purchased 13 Mack 1,000-gpm C95F triple combination pumpers in 1959. They were equipped with Waterous pumps, and 375-gallon booster tanks. A portable deluge nozzle was introduced in place of permanent deck pipes. Shown is FDNY Engine 275. (Photo courtesy Dick Adelman)

Baltimore purchased four identical Pirsch 1,000-gpm triple combination pumpers circa-1959. Second Line Engine 3 has a fixed turret pipe. Note windshield and covering for firefighters riding the tailboard. (Photo courtesy Dick Adelman)

In 1959, the San Jose Fire Department shops built this half-size American-LaFrance to use as a parade piece. (Photo courtesy Wayne Sorensen)

Circa-1960 American-LaFrance 900 series floodlight unit built for Odessa, New York. Similar body styles were used for rescue squads. Axes on the 900 series apparatus were usually mounted over the front fenders. (Photo courtesy American-LaFrance)

San Francisco's Engine 14 was a 1960 American-LaFrance 900 series 1,000-gpm triple combination powered by a Boeing 325-hp turbine engine. The turbine engine proved unreliable—it was noisy and lacked braking power. After three years, it was replaced with a Continental six-cylinder 330-hp gasoline engine. Above words "turbo chief" note the large, shiny exhaust, the size one associates with locomotives! Heat from the exhaust stack also caused close-by, overhanging, awnings to burst into flame. (Photo courtesy Wayne Sorensen)

Santa Clara, California, ran this 1960 American-LaFrance with a 1,250-gpm pump and a 500-gallon booster tank. In 1975, Van Pelt rebuilt the rig. (Photo courtesy Wayne Sorensen)

One of four 1960 Diamond T chassis used by Van Pelt to build 1,250-gpm triple combination pumpers for Oakland, California. This rig had a 300-gallon booster tank and a 100-gpm booster pump, and was powered by a Hall-Scott 320-hp engine. (Photo courtesy Wayne Sorensen)

One of two 1960 FWD 1,000-gpm triple combinations used in Baltimore. Unit is painted red and white. Firefighters riding on tailboard were protected by clear windshield and top. Shown is Engine 26. (Photo courtesy Wayne Sorensen)

Detroit, in 1960, received a FWD 1,000-gpm sedan pumper. (Photo courtesy Bill Friedrich)

A massive, 10,000-gpm deluge gun used by the Chicago Fire Department and mounted on a 1960 Reo all-wheel drive chassis. (Photo courtesy Wayne Sorensen)

Rear view shows some of the piping. (Photo courtesy Wayne Sorensen)

Oakland, California's Truck 1 was a 1960 Seagrave tractor, powered by a 935 G-1 Hall-Scott engine. The ladder was a three-section 100-foot metal aerial. (Photo courtesy Wayne Sorensen)

Cleveland, Ohio's elevating platform ran as Truck 16. The 1960 Sutphen tower has a telescopic lattice-type aluminum four-section boom. The boom was equipped with two turret nozzles. Note the Cincinnati cab and the tandem-axle chassis. Cincinnati cabs were supplied to a number of apparatus builders. (Photo courtesy Dick Adelman)

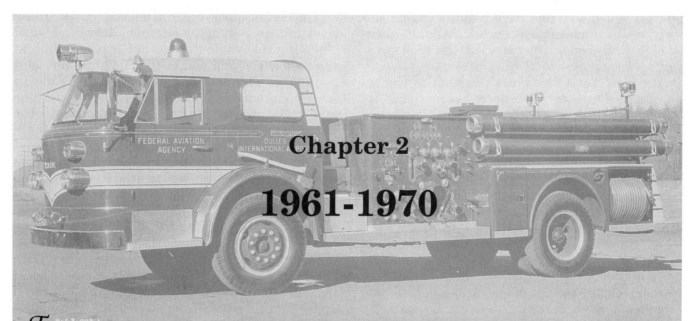

Chapter 2

1961-1970

$\mathcal{T}$he decade of the 1960s began in an upbeat mood with the inauguration of President John F. Kennedy. By the end of the decade there was an unpopular war in Southeast Asia and chaos in many of the nation's major cities. Riots occurred and, at first, police were targets of the rioters. Later firefighters, arriving to quell fires set by rioters, also became targets of rocks, bottles, debris and even Molotov cocktails. It was necessary to fit urban apparatus with plywood roofs to protect firefighters. Hose beds were also covered with fire-resistant material for protection from Molotov cocktails. By the end of the decade, new apparatus delivered had fully enclosed cabs and covers over most of the rigs' vulnerable spots. (Apparatus historians looking at this equipment a century from now will probably wonder why suddenly it became necessary to add these temporary roofs.)

Fire stations in major cities also kept their doors closed, to prevent missiles from being thrown inside. A secondary impact was that it made the fire house less accessible in that neighbors and small children couldn't wander in and out.

Affirmative action statutes were enacted that opened up employment opportunities for females and various minority groups. Integration of both females and minorities into many cities would not be accomplished easily and sometimes was accomplished only because of court orders. (As this book is being written, San Francisco's Chinese language cable channel is running commercials in Chinese attempting to interest women in ap-

plying for posts in the San Francisco Fire Department.)

During this decade FDNY purchased some elevating towers, and rebuilt a transit bus to carry firefighters. Some ex-military all-wheel drive Dodges were converted into brush rigs for use on Staten Island. In late-1963, FDNY signed a contract with Mack Trucks to build the equivalent of a land-based fireboat, capable of pumping prodigious amounts of water. It would be known as the Superpumper. The system, as it evolved, resulted in one large tractor-trailer pumper, a tractor-trailer tender carrying many needed parts, hose and fittings, three satellite pumpers that would get into position before the Superpumper arrived, and some hose relay trucks. The Superpumper was intended to take the place of 10 conventional pumpers at a fire site. An article in *Newsweek* exclaimed:

> Sucking water from rivers and harbors or from as many as four water mains at once, the huge fire engine could throw a stream of water nearly a quarter of a mile on level ground or 885 feet straight up—the height of the 74th floor of the Empire State Building. Shooting out 8,800 gallons per minute at a pressure of 350 pounds per square inch, the pumper could blast holes in brick walls—and if the wall is stubborn, the pressure could be boosted to 700 pounds.[1]

William Francis Gibbs gets much of the credit for designing the Superpumper; he was already a well-known naval architect and tried to build the land-bound equivalent of a fireboat. The Super-

---

[1] "A Fire Engine to Fight Flames 74 Floors High," *Newsweek* (July 22, 1963), p. 69.

pumper relied on a lightweight diesel engine and its hose was made of neoprene with a double jacket of polyethylene, necessary for the high pressures.

The New York Fire Patrol, one of the few remaining salvage corps in operation, reduced its number of stations, and switched to Chevrolets and Dodges, with enclosed bodies transferred from 1949 chassis. In 1970, Los Angeles converted one of its 1948 Mack salvage wagons into a helicopter tender.

In Arcadia, California, the dispatcher used a new type of machine called the "electrowriter" (apparently similar to today's FAX machines), which transmitted the dispatch orders in writing to the various fire companies. The receiving company would then push a button on their machine to acknowledge receipt of the message. This was considered more accurate than using voice. By the end of the decade, large departments were developing uses of mainframe computers to aid with dispatching. The computer's memory could be used to store information on the structure at each address, which would influence the equipment dispatched and could also be radioed to the captain of the company en route. After the fire was extinguished, information concerning its nature was added to the computer's database.

In 1963, Baltimore opened a new training center on a four-acre site. Its location was such that oil could be burned for training purposes without receiving complaints from neighbors. It was lit so it could be used at night, and had a 925-seat auditorium. The instructional buildings were large enough that pumpers and ladder trucks could be driven inside (and the vehicles' exhaust was vented). There was an enclosed chamber for gas training, as well as a conventional six-story training tower. Other facilities included a hose testing area, a drafting pit (for pump exercises), a high voltage grid (for demonstrating nozzle types to be used when near overhead wires), a large electric motor, a transformer, a tank car and an oil burner (all of which could be ignited inside and used for practicing how to combat fires in such settings). A 2-1/2 story "house" could be configured to represent a wide variety of firefighting situations. Lastly, there were some oil tank dikes, as one would encounter in a tank farm. One dike was square inside and one was circular inside; their shape determined firefighting strategy.[2]

The Tele-Squrt was introduced in 1970 and soon appeared on many pumpers. It was a 50-foot elevating telescopic device that was mounted at the rear of the pumper. (Other heights were also available.) The pedestal upon which the device was mounted was attached to the truck's frame and two outriggers were also attached to the truck's frame. As the Tele-Squrt expanded, both an extension ladder and a telescopic "waterway" extended as an integral part of it. The literature used the term "waterway" to describe telescoping pipes that extended with the ladder. The pipes took the place of hose that traditionally had been attached to the nozzle carried at the top of most ladders. In essence, the device was a 50-foot aerial ladder and water tower. Literature read: "With only three men, it can lay its own lines, boost pressure to the boom tip nozzle and deliver a 1,000-gpm fire quenching stream. . . ."[3] Note the reference to a crew of "three men"; the builder was conscious of the fact that many departments were running apparatus with smaller crews.

Squrt units could be controlled by a wireless remote control similar to the TV remote control "clickers" with which most of us are familiar. The Squrt unit was also designed so that it could be retrofitted onto many existing makes and models of pumpers, upgrading their capability without requiring the purchase of new apparatus. Tele-Squrt literature for its 65-foot model proclaimed: "Small volunteer and large metropolitan fire departments alike are discovering that the Tele-Squrt 65 delivers the firefighting and rescue capabilities they need with a one-time capital investment."

At the 1968 International Association of Fire Chiefs Conference in San Francisco, a snorkel tower was shown that carried a closed-circuit TV system. The camera was carried on the snorkel platform and had a wide-angle lens with a zoom feature. The camera could be controlled either by the fireman in the tower, or remotely from the ground. The monitor was at the base of the platform although the signal could be transmitted by cable to a nearby command post.[4]

In the late-1960s, there were major changes in the types of fire extinguishers that could be used, including those routinely carried on apparatus. The traditional soda-acid was found to be dangerous because sometimes the soda and acid did not mix thoroughly and, for a short period of time, the

---

[2] *The American City* (July 1963), p. 91.

[3] Literature published by Snorkel, a division of ATO, Inc. St. Joseph, Missouri, 1978.

[4] *The American City* (August 1968), p. 28.

device was passing acid out the nozzle. Carbon tetrachloride extinguishers, used for electrical fires, were abandoned because one of the gases they emitted was phosgene, which was dangerous to humans. By 1972, these two extinguishers, which accounted for about three-quarters of extinguishers in use, had to be removed from service. Today's apparatus carries extinguishers that are loaded with sodium bicarbonate, potassium bicarbonate, ammonium phosphate, or some combination thereof.

This was the decade when many departments switched to diesels. The fire chief in Albuquerque reported that the difference between diesel and gasoline was "in the maintenance requirements. On fire apparatus, gasoline engines require major tune-ups twice a year to ensure quick starts and dependable operation. This means replacing all dual ignition parts—12 spark plugs, two distributors, two sets of coils and wiring, besides tuning the engine.... With the diesel we change the lube and oil filters three times a year. That's all."[5] Spokane discovered that it had to install filters on its stations' fuel tanks because the diesel fuel, when placed in tanks that had held leaded gasoline, developed moisture that triggered an acid reaction that loosened lead particles from the sides of the tanks. These particles would clog the diesel engines' fuel injectors.[6]

American-LaFrance introduced an experimental Turbo-Jet in the early-1960s, and one saw service in San Francisco. It was not reliable and its engine both lacked braking ability going down hills (important in San Francisco) and was sluggish when starting out and going up hills (also important in San Francisco). The truck looked like a conventional 900 series except for a stainless steel exhaust stack at the top of the engine. Hot fumes from this exhaust melted overhead wires and ignited overhanging roofs and awnings. In 1964, a conventional gasoline engine was installed, replacing the turbine powered unit. In 1962, American-LaFrance introduced trucks with elevating platforms of lengths of 70, 80, and 90 feet. In 1965, the "Pioneer" line was introduced. These models were lower priced, and were an attempt to reach a wider market. During this decade diesels were increasingly popular powerplants for American-LaFrance and many other makes of apparatus.

Crown spent a busy decade supplying apparatus to Los Angeles and its surrounding cities. In 1963, it delivered to Los Angeles two manifold wagons, each equipped with 2,000-gpm pumps, a power-operated 2,000-gpm Stang turret, and 14 2-1/2-inch hose inlets. The trucks carried both 2-1/2 and 3-1/2-inch hose. Later in the decade Crown delivered to Los Angeles a wrecker/recovery vehicle with Holmes twin booms, a Pitman 85-foot snorkel, and two tractor-drawn Maxim 75-foot aerials. In addition to Los Angeles city and county, other large cities taking deliveries from Crown during this decade included: Berkeley, Honolulu, Oakland, Ogden, Phoenix, San Diego, Tacoma, and Tucson.

L.N. Curtis continued to outfit apparatus on chassis provided by both commercial truck builders plus Maxim and Ward LaFrance.

Further mention should be made of a firm that is still in existence, the W.S. Darley & Co., of Melrose Park, Illinois, founded in 1908. The firm initially was a catalog supplier of equipment used by municipalities. This included fire extinguishers, turnout gear, etc. By the late-1920s it was selling, on a piece-by-piece basis, all the equipment needed to convert a commercial chassis into a fire engine or ladder truck. It was the main supplier to those who built apparatus in local shops. In the mid-1930s, Darley began outfitting commercial chassis on its own, which it still does. Its main customers were, and continue to be, small community fire departments. However, some Darley-built equipment does show up in big city rosters, with examples being brush rigs, specialized hose wagons, tankers, and rescue squads. Private industrial fire brigades often use Darley equipment.

The Firebird elevating platform was introduced by the Calavar Corp., of Santa Fe Springs, California, in 1969. It was available in lengths of 90, 125, and 150 feet. The prototype was mounted on a FWD cab-forward chassis and sold to Philadelphia.

FMC moved its John Bean high-pressure pump manufacturing operation to Tipton, Indiana. Its pumps produced fog that was effective in smothering fire and left less water damage. During World War II, the Navy had found fog systems to be effective for fighting shipboard fires.

FWD produced cab-forward chassis that were used by a number of apparatus outfitters for mounting ladders and elevating platforms. Conventional FWD chassis were used to carry pumper bodies, with sales made mainly to northern

[5] *The American City* (November 1971), p. 36.
[6] *The American City* (November 1970), p. 48.

cities that wanted the truck's superior traction. In a big move, FWD acquired Seagrave in 1963.

Hahn concentrated on building custom apparatus. It also sold chassis to other outfitters such as Superior and Van Pelt.

In 1961, Howe took over Oren-Roanoke and its plant in Vinton, Virginia. In 1965, Howe acquired Coast Apparatus, Inc., in Martinez, California. In 1966, Howe introduced the top-mounted control panel for the pump operator, a feature found on many apparatus today. The operator stands between the cab and hose bed and can see 360 degrees, and is also protected from traffic on the street. Howe outfitted many pumpers on Ford C chassis.

Mack made many deliveries to large cities during this decade, and pushed the use of diesel, rather than gasoline, power. Mack introduced its Aerialscope, which had a working elevation of 75 feet. It had four different functions: (1) water tower, (2) exterior elevator to carry firefighters, equipment, or rescued individuals, (3) observation post, and (4) rescue platform capable of reaching individual windows. In 1970, Mack delivered six Mack chassis to the Chicago Fire Department, where they were outfitted by the Truck Body Co. (in Chicago) with rescue squad bodies. They were used to carry flying squads of additional firefighters to large fires where they supplemented firefighters already on the scene.

Maxim sold four 100-foot tractor-drawn aerials to Philadelphia in 1961. During this decade it produced a wide range of apparatus types including brush rigs, snorkels, and tankers. Its major market continued to be the Northeast.

Oren-Roanoke was turning out apparatus on Duplex, Ford, and International chassis. In the New Jersey area, Oren apparatus was sold under the name "Great Eastern," by the New Jersey Fire Equipment Co., of Dunellen.

Pierce continued to build apparatus on commercial chassis, and to build fire apparatus bodies for use by others. It made a number of sales to Chicago.

Pirsch introduced its cab-forward models in 1962. During the decade the firm—which remained family-owned—sold many aerial ladders and elevating platforms, as well as conventional pumpers.

Sanford, a small firm located in Syracuse since 1912 where it originally produced commercial trucks, was turning out apparatus on Ford and International chassis. In the mid-1960s, it offered custom models on Duplex chassis and in 1969 offered the option of diesel power.

Seagrave was purchased by FWD in 1963 and between 1963 and 1965, the operation was moved from Columbus, Ohio, to Clintonville, Wisconsin. FWD already was a builder of fire apparatus, although it was dependent upon more outside suppliers than was Seagrave. No doubt much of the later half of the decade was devoted to integrating the operations of two small producers of high-quality products. FWD continued to supply chassis to other apparatus builders. In 1963, Seagrave did introduce a rear-mount aerial, called the "rear admiral."

The Sutphen firm, in Springfield, Ohio, had been formed in 1890 and was a small producer of firefighting apparatus. In the mid-1960s, the firm introduced its own aerial tower, which had the waterway and hydraulic lifts inside the boom/ladder. It was available in lengths of 65, 75, and 85 feet. The firm was reaching out into national markets, similar to other firms that barely deserved mention up to this time.

Towers Fire Apparatus Co., of Freeburg, Illinois, founded in 1946, delivered a snorkel to St. Louis, Missouri. The firm had also built some aircraft rescue vehicles for McDonnell Aircraft, consisting of an elevating ladder carried on a Jeep chassis.

In 1961, Van Pelt used an all-wheel drive Oshkosh chassis to build a pumper for Palo Alto. Later in the decade, Van Pelt supplied several pieces of apparatus to Oakland, including that city's first diesels. Van Pelt also used Duplex chassis.

Ward LaFrance had introduced its "Firebrand" line in 1960, based on a cab-forward design. In 1962, the Firebrand was replaced with the "Mark I," and in 1965, the firm sold its first elevating platform. During the decade, the firm made large sales to cities in the Northeast, plus Detroit, Chicago, and Memphis. The firm also built a number of airport crash trucks that were sold throughout the United States. During this decade, Ward LaFrance and Maxim merged.

At the end of the decade, when one looks at the industry, he or she sees a nearly full deck of apparatus builders. Many of the established old line builders were located in aging facilities and saddled with high labor costs. Their fine reputations would carry them for another decade or two, but there is no question that they were in decline. By 1996, only FWD and Seagrave would survive as firms that were considered as major builders in Volume One of this study. Mack, as a producer of trucks, also survives although it no longer builds fire apparatus itself.

Campbell, California's 1961 American-LaFrance, Model D-910-PKO, 900 series 1,000-gpm pumper taking water from a hydrant using soft suction hose. Demonstration took place at "pump-in" at Livermore, California, June 4, 1994. (Photo courtesy Wayne Sorensen)

A 1961 Coast Custom 1,250-gpm pumper with a 300-gallon booster tank. It's shown in 1977 as a reserve rig in Sacramento. (Photo courtesy Wayne Sorensen)

A 1961 Crown/Pitman Snorkel with a 1,250-gpm, two-stage Waterous pump. The articulating boom has two sections, totaling 85 feet in length. It was used in Oakland, California. (Photo courtesy Wayne Sorensen)

In 1961, Ford's new C Series tilt-cabs were an instant success in fire apparatus and many other markets. American-LaFrance built a large fleet of these engines for San Jose. Shown is Engine 18. They were 750-gpm and 1,000-gpm pumpers, all with 500-gallon booster tanks. The Federal Q siren is mounted on the nose. The short wheelbase sacrificed no carrying capacity. (Photo courtesy Wayne Sorensen)

A Dutch-made Geesink rear-mount 85-foot aerial ladder was placed on a 1961 FWD chassis for Milwaukee's Ladder 2. (Photo courtesy Dick Adelman)

Indianapolis used this 1961 International with a Holmes twin-boom wrecker body to service its fleet. (Photo courtesy Dick Adelman)

The Chicago Fire Department purchased two Jeep FC-170 chassis in 1961. Special smoke ejector bodies and equipment for these chassis were built by John Bean, of Lansing, Michigan. The large, round tubs are accordion-folding smoke pipes that attach to the round connection on the side of the apparatus. Deadly smoke and gases are cleared out of buildings by a powerful motor. (Photo courtesy Dick Adelman)

As the Maxim distributor for the Pacific Northwest, L.N. Curtis ordered a Maxim F chassis to be completed by Heiser Body Co. of Seattle. Parkland, Washington, purchased this cab-forward 1961, 1,250-gpm triple combination with a 600-gallon water tank. It has a five-man canopy cab. (Photo courtesy Bill Hattersley)

This 1961 Maxim 100-foot aerial ladder was one of four sold to Philadelphia. Cab roof and shielding around tiller were added later. (Photo courtesy Dan G. Martin)

A 1961 Pirsch 1,500-gpm triple combination purchased by Memphis. The suction hose is carried squirrel tail around the front of the engine. It was equipped with a four-door cab and fixed turret pipe. Photo taken as reserve engine January 18, 1980. (Photo courtesy Wayne Sorensen)

This 1961 Seagrave was Cincinnati's Engine 12. Siren and red light are mounted above cab instead of inside the hole in the hood, above the grille, where the siren was usually placed. The result was that this piece of apparatus was nicknamed "Rudolph." (Photo courtesy Dick Adelman)

Baltimore had two identical 1961 Ward LaFrance 1,000-gpm pumpers. Engine 18 has a semi-cab and a Federal Q siren mounted on the fender. (Photo courtesy Dick Adelman)

A 1962 American-LaFrance Airport Chief operated by the Federal Aviation Agency at Washington D.C.'s Dulles International Airport. Notice the high visibility reflectorized band around the middle of the cab and on the cab roof. (Photo courtesy American-LaFrance)

San Francisco, California's Truck 7 operated this 1962 900 series American-LaFrance 100-foot metal aerial. Initially, it was powered by a six-cylinder Continental 330-hp engine, but around 1970 it was converted to a Detroit six-cylinder, 219-hp diesel. Tractor had a half-cab, later converted to full. Aerial had hill table-leveling device, necessary in San Francisco. The outriggers were manually operated. (Photo courtesy Wayne Sorensen)

One of six Coast Custom Model 1500 pumpers placed in-service in 1962 by Sacramento. Shown is Engine 6 equipped with a 1,250-gpm Waterous pump and 300-gallon water tank. (Photo courtesy Edward W. Gardiner)

A 1962 Dodge P series chassis used by American-LaFrance to build this 1,000-gpm pumper for Darien, New York. It had a 500-gallon booster tank. (Photo courtesy Roland Boulet)

Vernon, California, bought this 1962 Ford/Van Pelt with an 85-foot Hi-Ranger snorkel-type platform. Note large outriggers on each side of ground ladder. (Photo courtesy Van Pelt)

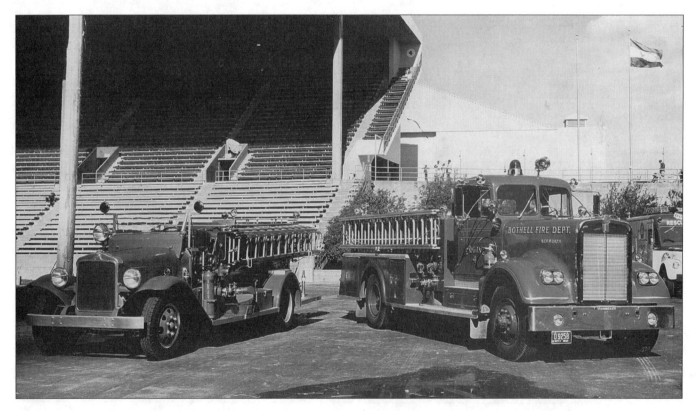

On right is Bothell, Washington's 1962 Kenworth with a 1,500-gpm Hale pump. Left is Kenworth's first fire chassis, delivered to Sumner, Washington, in 1932 and still used as a parade piece. Photo taken at Seattle's World Fair in 1962. Note how much larger the newer apparatus is. (Photo courtesy Kenworth)

Some colleges and universities operate their own fire departments. Stanford University located near Palo Alto, California, is one example. This 1962 straight-frame 85-foot Seagrave Anniversary Series has squared front fenders. (Photo courtesy Wayne Sorensen)

A 1962 Van Pelt Custom 75-foot Hi-Ranger Snorkel. The six-wheel chassis and entire body were built by Van Pelt. Unit has a five-man cab and the power is Hall-Scott engine. In service in Redwood City, California. (Photo courtesy Wayne Sorensen)

Boston received 10 of these 1962 Ward LaFrance 1,000-gpm pumpers with a fixed turret pipe. This was Wagon 39. It has a semi-cab with a protective cover over the crew seat and over the rear step due to civil unrest. (Photo courtesy Dick Adelman)

Lockheed-Georgia Co., in Marietta, Georgia, an aircraft builder, operated this 1963 Autocar tractor that pulled a trailer unit built by Howe. The truck tractor had a 320-hp diesel engine. There are two pumping units, one at each end of the trailer, and there are also Cardox 6,000-gpm foam-making machines at each end of the trailer. The three-axle trailer carried 10,000 gallons of water and 1,000 gallons of foam. On its roof are Cardox foam turrets. A 10,000-watt generator supplies power for lights and rescue equipment. (Photo courtesy Volvo/White)

Mountain View, California, used this 1963 Crown Firecoach Model CS 75-81, 75-foot snorkel. This snorkel was photographed in parade on August 20, 1988. (Photo courtesy Wayne Sorensen)

Ogden, Utah, bought this 1963 Crown Firecoach with an 85-foot snorkel. The five-man half-cab was ahead of front axle. Rig had dual A-frame outriggers that were self-leveling and self-locking. (Photo courtesy Wayne Sorensen)

A 1963 Maxim Model S 100-foot tractor-drawn aerial. In-service as Truck 7, in Louisville. (Photo courtesy Dick Adelman)

St. Louis used this 1964 Central, built by the Central Fire Truck Corp. of St. Louis and Manchester, Missouri, on a FWD chassis. It had a 1,000-gpm pump. (Photo courtesy Robert Pauly)

One of four identical heavy-duty Diamond T chassis used by Van Pelt to build 1,250-gpm pumpers for Oakland, California. Shown is an open-cab pumper of Engine 9 equipped with a 300-gallon booster tank and 100-gpm booster pump. The unit's power was a Hall-Scott 6182 six-cylinder 320-hp gasoline engine. (Photo courtesy Wayne Sorensen)

Birmingham, Alabama, Engine 14 ran this 1964 FWD/Central. Central Fire Truck Corp. outfitted the pumper's body. (Photo courtesy Wayne Sorensen)

This 1964 FWD with a 1,000-gpm pump and 65-foot Pitman Snorkel was used in Paterson, New Jersey. It had a Cincinnati canopy cab. (Photo courtesy Dick Adelman)

Engine Company 1 of Asbury Park, New Jersey, operated this 1,000-gpm triple combination 1964 Hahn canopy cab-forward pumper. (Photo courtesy Jim Burner Jr.)

The Dupo Fire Protection District in Illinois used this large 1964 Howe built on a Duplex chassis. The pump was rated at 750 gpm, and the water tank held 500 gallons. (Photo courtesy Dick Adelman)

A 1964 Curtis-Heiser 1,500-gpm triple combination built on a Kenworth enclosed cab model. Built for King County Fire District No. 14, Washington. The pumper has a 240-gallon water tank. The power was a 300-hp gasoline Hall-Scott engine. (Photo courtesy Kenworth Motor Truck Co.)

Photographed in front of Crown's Los Angeles plant was this 85-foot Pitman Snorkel built for use in Honolulu. Chassis is a 1964 International. (Photo courtesy Crown)

Louisville's Engine 16's 1964 Maxim Model S 1,250-gpm triple combination. The pumper has a semi-cab with squirrel tail hard suction hose. (Photo courtesy Dick Adelman)

Seattle used this 1964 Maxim "F" Series cab-forward truck with a 100-foot metal, four-section hydraulically operated aerial ladder. Rig was powered by a Hall-Scott 330-hp engine. First assignment Ladder 9, shown as Ladder 7. (Photo courtesy Bill Hattersley)

A circa-1964 Pirsch with a Pitman Snorkel, offering a good view of the booms at a working fire. The operator in the platform, or basket, can change both his position and direction of the stream of water. A-frame outriggers are visible. (Photo courtesy Kenosha Historical Society.)

A 1965 American-LaFrance 900 series 1,250-gpm half-cab pumper built for Engine 2 in Anchorage, Alaska. It has a heated 300-gallon booster tank. The electronic siren is mounted on top of the bumper. (Photo courtesy Wayne Sorensen)

This 1965 Coast 1,000-gpm triple combination was built for Sunnyvale, California. Shown is Engine 3, one of three identical pumpers with International cabs and chassis with sheet metal by Coast. (Photo courtesy Wayne Sorensen)

A 1965 Crown CP-125-109, 1,250-gpm pumper with a 300-gallon booster tank, which ran as Engine 1 in Oakland, California. The pump was a Waterous. (Photo courtesy Wayne Sorensen)

This 1960s Ford C chassis carried a 65-foot Pitman Snorkel and was used in Amarillo, Texas. The truck's windshield was cut into to reduce the rig's height. Also carried were 208 feet of ground ladders. (Photo courtesy Allegheny Fire Equipment Co.)

A 1965 Ford C chassis used by the Boardman Co. of Oklahoma City to build a 500-gpm pumper that was later converted to Cave-in Rescue by the Phoenix Fire Department. Note front suction and bumper air horn location. Above cab is a speaker that amplifies radio so it can he heard outside cab. (Photo courtesy Bill Hattersley)

Fire Associations of Santa Clara Valley Support Unit One donated by Mountain View's Department in 1978, where it had run as Rescue 50. This 1965 unit is housed at Santa Clara City Fire Station 9. The purpose of fire associates is to provide short term canteen service for any official call from a fire department in Santa Clara Valley. Units are radio called by fire departments for services at multiple alarm fires. (Photo courtesy Wayne Sorensen)

Central Fire Truck Corp. of St. Louis used a 1965 FWD chassis to build a 1,000-gpm pumper later converted to use as Foam 7 by the fire department in that city. (Photo courtesy Dick Adelman)

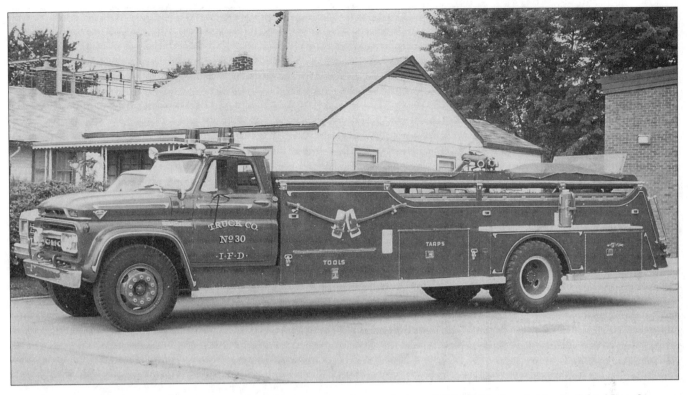

The Indianapolis Fire Department shops built this city service truck on a 1965 GMC chassis. A windshield at the rear protects those standing on rear step. (Photo courtesy Dick Adelman)

A 1965 Hahn custom cab-forward 1,000-gpm triple combination used by Marley Park, Maryland. (Photo courtesy Dick Adelman)

Howe Fire Equipment circa-1965 Model HR-72 on an International C08190 Special Fire Chassis, delivered to Lykens, Pennsylvania. The pumper is equipped with a Waterous 750-gpm two-stage pump, 500-gallon water tank, and a Howe electric hose reel. (Photo courtesy Howe Fire Apparatus Co.)

The Sanford Motor Truck Co. of Syracuse, New York, used an International "S" series conventional chassis to build Ogdensburg, New York's 1965 1,000-gpm triple combination. (Photo courtesy William F. Adams)

Missoula bought this 1965 Mack 75-foot Aerialscope, which utilized a telescopic boom. Stabilizer jacks are located at front, middle, and rear. (Photo courtesy Bill Hattersley)

The concept of a "superpumper" was conceived by William Francis Gibbs, a well-known naval architect and marine engineer. During 1962, Mack Trucks was invited by FDNY to participate in the design of the Superpumper and a tender. The photo shows a demonstration of the Superpumper in the foreground and three Mack satellite tenders. (Photo courtesy FDNY)

The tractor used for the FDNY Superpumper is a commercial Mack cab-over-engine model F715STP. The engine is a Mack diesel of 255 hp. An Allison six-speed semi-automatic transmission coupled to the engine is equipped to drive the priming pump and start the air compressor for the pump engine. Mounted at the rear of the trailer is the Delaval six stage, 8,800-gpm pump. Coupled to the pump is the Napier-Deltic diesel engine. (Photo courtesy FDNY)

Another view of Mack's FDNY land-based mobile pumping system. Twelve-inch suction hose is carried beneath the engine access doors in the trailer. A mechanical crane at the rear of the trailer is used to support suction hose when drafting. (Photo courtesy Dick Adelman)

Mack built three Model C85FD cab forward satellite tenders for the FDNY Superpumper System, powered by Mack's 176-hp diesel engine. The hose bed contained 2,000 feet of 4-1/2-inch hose. The unit had a Stang "Intelligiant" monitor with a capacity of 4,000 gpm. The satellite had four inlets, two on each side. Shown is Satellite 3. (Photo courtesy Dick Adelman)

Mack also built a single tender to accompany the Superpumper. The tractor used for the FDNY Superpumper's tender was the commercial Mack cab over engine model. The tender carried 2,000 feet of 4-1/2-inch line. The tractor was equipped with a platform to support a large Stang "Intelligiant" monitor with an eight-inch barrel operated by hand wheels and a 2,000-gpm fog tip. The tractor was designed to be detached at the fire scene. There were hydraulically operated outriggers on each side of the cab. (Photo courtesy Wayne Sorensen)

Circa-1965 Mack/Gerstenslager rescue, with body fabricated by Gerstenslager Corp. of Wooster, Ohio. Rescue unit operated by West Hempstead, New York. Built on Mack C chassis, frequently regarded as one of the best looking cab forward designs of that era. Note twin siren-warning lights on roof. (Photo courtesy Gerstenslager)

This 1965 Maxim "S" 1,000-gpm triple combination pumper ran as Engine 27 in Indianapolis. (Photo courtesy Dan G. Martin)

Haddonfield, New Jersey's 750-gpm 1965 Oren appears in a parade. It was built on a Duplex chassis. (Photo courtesy Jim Burner)

Syracuse ran this rescue squad that utilized a Gerstenslager body on a 1965 Seagrave chassis. A-frame in front of truck is for lifting and towing. A loudspeaker is mounted above cab, below rotating beacon. (Photo courtesy Dick Adelman)

Cleveland operated this 1965 Ward LaFrance 65-foot snorkel. Note low profile cab. The truck also carried a full complement of ground ladders. (Photo courtesy Dick Adelman)

A 1966 American-LaFrance Series 100, full-cab 100-foot aerial running as Truck 1 in Anchorage, Alaska. It has manual stabilizer jacks. (Photo courtesy Wayne Sorensen)

Some of the largest of apparatus in use are water tankers. This is a 1966 Brockway tractor pulling a 5,000-gallon trailer, used in Pedricktown, New Jersey. (Photo courtesy Ray Stevens)

A 1966 Coast Custom engine-ahead 1,250-gpm triple combination started by Coast and finished by Howe. The chassis was an International. The pumper had a 1,250-gpm Waterous pump and the truck carried 500 gallons of water. The pumper was built for Brisbane, California. (Photo courtesy Wayne Sorensen)

A 1966 Ford tilt-cab 1,000-gpm triple combination pumper built for Clinton, Maryland, and later sold to the Harry Lundberg School at Piney Point, Maryland. Note the two-windshield cab. (Photo courtesy Dick Adelman)

This circa-1966 Pierce was built on a FWD chassis and delivered to Bloomington, Minnesota. It had a 1,000-gpm pump and a Cincinnati cab. (Photo courtesy Pierce)

Washington, D.C. purchased a 1966 Pirsch 750-gpm conventional triple combination pumper assigned to Engine 5. The pumper is equipped with front suction. Note the riot plywood cab covering. (Photo courtesy Dick Adelman)

Fair Oaks, California, bought this 1966 Van Pelt Custom, built on a Duplex chassis. (Photo courtesy Van Pelt)

American-LaFrance built its first Aerialscope in 1962. This 1967, 90-foot Custom Aero Chief was purchased by Santa Clara. It was powered by a Continental Red Seal six-cylinder, 305-hp gasoline engine. (Photo courtesy Wayne Sorensen)

San Francisco's Truck 10 was a 1967 American-LaFrance tractor powered by a Continental six-cylinder, 330-hp engine. The trailer had a 100-foot aerial with a hill-table leveling device with four manually-operated outriggers. The aerial had a ladder pipe attachment. This was the first unit in San Francisco to have a fully enclosed cab and enclosed tiller seat. (Photo courtesy Wayne Sorensen)

Atlanta's Truck 1 was pulled by a 1967 Ford C tractor with an extended cab. The aerial ladder was a 100-foot Pirsch. (Photo courtesy Dick Adelman)

Cleveland's Engine 11, mounted on a Ford C chassis, is shown in action. The rear-mounted suction hose is in use and the monitor on the hose bed directs a stream of water through the burning structure's window. (Photo courtesy John Systma)

Lawrence, Massachusetts, purchased this 1967 Young-Pitman 75-foot snorkel on a FWD chassis. (Photo courtesy Dick Adelman)

New Market, New Jersey, ran this 1967 Great Eastern custom 750-gpm pumper. (Photo courtesy Ernest N. Day)

One of four 1967 custom Howe Duplex 1,000-gpm triple combinations delivered to Sacramento. These canopy cab-forward pumpers also had 500-gallon water tanks. (Photo courtesy Howe Fire Apparatus Co.)

A 1967 Mack C957 cab-forward pumper used by Engine 27 in Denver. It has a 1,000-gpm pump and added compartments above rear wheels. (Photo courtesy Dick Adelman)

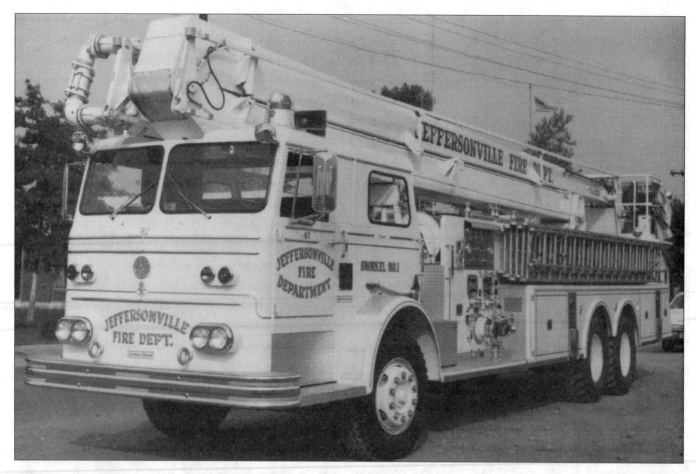

Jeffersonville, Kentucky, operated this 1967 Maxim that had a 75-foot Pitman Snorkel and a 1,000-gpm Hale pump. Tandem flotation tires were in the rear and power was a Cummins diesel. (Photo courtesy Dick Adelman)

This 1968 American-LaFrance triple-combination was used in Pittsburgh. Both front and rear axles were powered, giving it all-wheel drive capability. Note pre-connected hand lines. (Photo courtesy Dick Adelman)

A 1968 John Bean 1,250-gpm triple combination mounted on a Duplex chassis, powered by a Waukesha gasoline engine. It ran as Engine 1 in Peoria, Illinois.

This 1968 Crown was purchased by Los Angeles. It has Holmes Twin Boom wrecker cranes, plus an air compressor, and a generator. Originally it was powered by a Hall-Scott gasoline engine, which was later replaced by a Caterpillar diesel. (Photo courtesy Wayne Sorensen)

Divco was a well-known builder of stand-up milk delivery vans. This 1968 Divco was used in Albertson, Long Island, New York, as a squad. (Photo courtesy Jim Burness)

Hermiston, Oregon, ran this huge 1968 FWD outfitted by Western States with a 1,000-gpm pump and a 1,000-gallon tank. This rig was used to "chase" grass and grain fires. A firefighter rode in front behind the brush guard, with a hose line being fed from the booster tank. The hose is barely visible, in front of FWD emblem on side of hood. (Photo courtesy John W. Sorensen)

Yakima County, Washington, operated this 1968 FWD/Western States 750-gpm pumper that had a 1,000-gallon booster tank. Note pump controls and inlet in front. (Photo courtesy Bill Hattersley)

Hahn Motors, Inc. was located in Hamburg, Pennsylvania, and Hahn fire apparatus were not common on the West Coast. However, Portland, Oregon, ran this 1968 Hahn 1,250-gpm pumper with a 300-gallon booster tank as Engine 20. (Photo courtesy Bill Hattersley)

Pump panel of Mack CF 1,000-gpm pumper delivered to FDNY in 1968. (Photo courtesy Mack)

In 1968, New York City received 20 1,000-gpm pumpers, CF Models from Mack. They were delivered with "riot-gear" that included a rounded cover over the hose bed to protect the hose from Molotov cocktails and doors to cover the bucket seat behind the cab positions. The rear step was also protected. (Photo courtesy Mack)

A local firm, Van Buren, located in Mineola, New York, built this squad for East Meadow, New York, on a 1968 Mack F chassis. The unit has a 25-kw generator and a 10-ton front-mounted winch. (Photo courtesy Jim Burner Jr.)

L.N. Curtis was an apparatus outfitter as well as the longtime West Coast distributor for Maxim Motor Co. apparatus, built in Middleboro, Massachusetts. Sometimes Curtis bought Maxim chassis, which he then completed on the West Coast. This is one such example: a 1968 Maxim/Curtis/Heiser with the Heiser being the name of a well-known Seattle truck body builder. This vehicle was a 1,750-gpm triple-combination pumper and had a 500-gallon water tank. It ran in Burien, Washington, and was painted white. (Photo courtesy Bill Hattersley)

L.N. Curtis ordered this 1968 Maxim F chassis with a five-man canopy cab. The bodywork was done by Heiser. The pumper is shown in-service for Grant County Fire District No. 5 located at Moses Lake, Washington. The pumper has a 1,750-gpm pump and 500-gallon water tank. (Photo courtesy Bill Hattersley)

Oakland, California's first diesels were a pair of 1968 Van Pelt pumpers, one of which, Engine 16, is shown here. They had 1,250-gpm pumps plus separate 120-gpm booster pumps. Front suction hose is carried behind bumper. (Photo courtesy Wayne Sorensen)

A familiar 1969 American-LaFrance 900 series, diesel-powered 1,000-gpm triple combination. Built for Engine 6 of Baltimore. Note the dual headlights and the Federal Q siren mounted above the bumper. (Photo courtesy American-LaFrance)

The Texas Firemen's Training School at College Station used this 1969 John Bean 1,750-gpm pumper mounted on a Duplex chassis. (Photo courtesy Dick Adelman)

Ready for action is this 1969 Crown Firecoach rear-mount 100-foot Maxim aerial. It was Mountain View, California's Truck 51. The sign on the side reads: "A Smoke Detector Can Save Your Life." Photo taken February 20, 1978. (Photo courtesy Wayne Sorensen)

This 1969 Ford-Pirsch ran as the hose wagon half of a two-part Engine 5 Company in Washington, D.C. It had a 750-gpm pump and was built on a Ford F chassis. (Photo courtesy Dick Adelman)

One of two 1969 Ford-Maxim hose wagons purchased by Boston. The bodywork was by Pierce and the 50-foot articulating boom with a remote-controlled nozzle was supplied by Pittman. (Photo courtesy Dick Adelman)

The Calavar Corp. of Santa Fe Springs, California, placed its first Firebird elevating platform in-service in Philadelphia in 1969. The Firebird had a 125-foot boom and was the highest aerial platform produced in the United States. It was on a FWD chassis. (Photo courtesy Dan Martin)

A 1969 Great Eastern Custom, with a 1,000-gpm pump, built by Oren on a custom Duplex cab-forward chassis sold by Ernest Day's New Jersey Fire Equipment Co. to Runnemede, New Jersey. (Photo courtesy Wayne Sorensen)

Chicago purchased two International/Pierce Model CO 8190 cab-over-engine pumpers in 1969. Engine 25 is shown here; it's equipped with a 1,000-gpm Waterous pump and 500-gallon booster tank. (Photo courtesy Bob Freeman/Dick Adelman)

One of two International Model Co. 8190 1,000-gpm pumpers delivered to Chicago by Pierce in 1969. Engine 30 was powered by an International V-8 gasoline engine. (Photo courtesy Dick Adelman)

The King County Fire District 16 in Kenmore, Washington, ran this 1969 Kenworth 900 series Curtis-Heiser with a 1,750-gpm pump and 300-gallon booster tank. An 8V-71 Detroit diesel powered the rig. (Photo courtesy Kenworth)

In July 1969, Mack entered into contract with Baker Equipment Engineering Co. to design and produce the Aerialscope on a Mack Model CF chassis. This one was used in Cheltenham, Pennsylvania.

One of a group of five pumpers delivered to Pittsburgh is this 1969 Mack R Series. Shown is Engine 8, a 1,250-gpm triple combination pumper. The pumper has a standard closed cab. (Photo courtesy Dick Adelman)

This low-profile 1969 Pierce 1,250-gpm triple combination on an Oshkosh chassis was used in Chicago. Power was a Detroit diesel. The operator's panel was covered with black vinyl. (Photo courtesy Dick Adelman)

In 1969, Sanford was offering custom chassis apparatus on the Duplex chassis. Shown is Brewerton, New York's 1,250-gpm combination cab-forward canopy cab pumper. (Photo courtesy Sanford Fire Apparatus)

Sanford, in 1969, delivered to Syracuse this 1,500-gpm triple combination Duplex cab-forward chassis with a five-man Cincinnati cab. The pumper's power is a Detroit diesel engine. (Photo courtesy Dan G. Martin)

Rescue 1 in St. Louis was mounted on a 1969 Seagrave chassis with bodywork by Marion. (Photo courtesy Dick Adelman)

A 1970 American-LaFrance 100-foot aerial used in Boston. Tiller cab is enclosed. (Photo courtesy American-LaFrance)

A 1970 American-LaFrance Pioneer 2 pumper purchased by Santa Clara. It was equipped with a 1,250-gpm pump and 500-gallon booster tank. Power was from a Detroit 8V-71 diesel engine. Note pre-connected front suction hose. (Photo courtesy Wayne Sorensen)

Seattle, Washington, in 1970 purchased a 900 series, enclosed cab American-LaFrance, six-wheel chassis, 80-foot "Aero Chief" hydraulically-operated elevating platform truck. It proved to be unsuccessful. In 1976, the truck was sent to Maxim to have the elevating platform removed and replaced with a Maxim 100-foot rear-mount ladder aerial. In service as Truck 7, and as Truck 5. (Photo courtesy Paul Darrell)

A 1970 Caterpillar-Klein crash rig at McCarran International Airport in Clark County, Nevada. This rig pumps 1,800 gpm, pulls a 7,000-gallon tank of water and carries a foam system. It has two fixed turret pipes on platform above water tank. (Photo courtesy Bill Friedrich)

Hahn also built some apparatus on commercial chassis. Shown is Frederica, Delaware's 1970 Ford C tilt-cab 750-gpm triple combination with a 750-gallon water tank. (Photo courtesy Wayne Sorensen)

Sudlersville, Maryland, purchased this 1970 deluxe Ford C pumper from Oren. Many of Oren's customers purchased Oren apparatus on commercial chassis. The Ford tilt-cab was popular with its customers. Sudlersville's pumper was a 1,000-gpm triple combination with a 1,000-gallon water tank. (Photo courtesy Ray Stevens)

Some cities purchased commercial truck tractors to meet budget restrictions. Shown is Cleveland's 1970 Pirsch 100-foot Senior aerial pulled by a GMC tractor with a five-man canopy cab. Note the open tiller seat. (Photo courtesy Dick Adelman)

In 1970, Hahn Motors built 14 of these custom pumpers for Boston. They had 1,250-gpm pumps and Cincinnati cabs. At front is pre-connected soft suction hose. At top is a portable monitor and pre-connected 1-1/2-inch attack lines are visible in the side beds. (Photo courtesy Dick Adelman)

The Geo. Heiser Body Co. of Seattle, Washington, started building fire apparatus on commercial chassis about 1940. It also did bodywork for other apparatus outfitters. Shown is a 1970 Kenworth and Hale 1,750-gpm pump going through pump tests. (Photo courtesy Heiser Body Co.)

Seattle's 1970 Kenworth/Curtis with a 1,750-gpm Hale pump. A triple combination pumper, Engine 24 has a Stang monitor. Rig is equipped with 400-gallon booster tank, and a fixed 3,000-gpm monitor. It was purchased through L.N. Curtis Co. with bodywork by Heiser. In 1989, a prefabricated open crew cab was installed. There is a portable, plastic crew cab roof installed that can be removed for operation of the monitor. Hard suctions and suction brackets were removed. Ladder brackets and ladders were moved to former hard suction location on apparatus. Ladder brackets were replaced with breathing apparatus compartments. (Photo courtesy Bill Hattersley)

Seattle displayed the new and the old. On right is a 1970 Kenworth/Curtis, powered by a Detroit diesel engine and carrying a 1,750-gpm pump. Left is a 1916 Seagrave tractor installed in front of a 1907 American-LaFrance "Metropolitan" 700-gpm steam-powered pump. Note hose reel on steamer with small diameter hose. That was used for extinguishing fires started by the steamer's sparks. (Photo courtesy Seattle Fire Department)

One of six 1970 Mack MB Series chassis with bodywork by the Truck Body Co. built for Chicago. Rescue-type bodies were mounted on these chassis and the units assigned to Flying Squads created to supplement manpower at working fires. (Photo courtesy Bill Friedrich)

Newport, Rhode Island, received this 1970 Maxim Model F cab-forward. The 1,000-gpm triple combination had a roof turret and a Rockwood Foam System. (Photo courtesy Dick Adelman)

A 1970 Pirsch custom four-door, 1,250-gpm pumper in-service in Minneapolis. Note the sand boxes and sanders in front of rear wheels. (Photo courtesy Walt Schryver)

Oakland, California, placed this 1970 Seagrave with a 100-foot aerial in-service as Truck 7. A 350-hp Detroit V-8 diesel powered the rig. (Photo courtesy Wayne Sorensen)

One of two Sutphen quints with 85-foot elevating platforms delivered to Citrus Heights, California, in 1970. The quint had a 1,000-gpm Hale pump, a 300-gallon water tank, and 290 feet of ground ladders. (Photo courtesy Wayne Sorensen)

Santa Maria, California, ran this 1970 Van Pelt Custom 1,250-gpm triple combination pumper that was built on a Duplex chassis. (Photo courtesy Van Pelt)

In 1970, Ward LaFrance delivered five Grove rear-mounted 100-foot aerials to Chicago. Note the booster reel above the ground ladders. The trucks were equipped with 250-gallon booster tanks. The power was the Detroit 8V-71 diesel. (Photo courtesy Bill Friedrich)

Louisville operated this 1970 Ward LaFrance Ambassador model 1,000-gpm triple combination pumper. Pump had front suction with bin for holding soft suction hose, and an interesting squirrel tail mount for the suction hose above the rear wheel. (Photo courtesy Dick Adelman)

Chapter 3

1971-1980

$\mathcal{D}$ual airhorns were mounted on some apparatus and were used when approaching intersections. Grand Rapids, Michigan, installed a traffic control system manufactured by 3M called "Opticom." It consisted of an emitter, which was a small, flashing white strobe light on the top of the fire truck, a detector mounted over the intersection, which could "sense" when the flashing white strobe light was approaching, and a phase selector box inside the control box that would have the light turn the traffic signals green in the direction the fire truck was traveling. When a fire crew approached an intersection with the device and it would not give them a green light, it was because another piece of fire apparatus was approaching from a side street and the device gave them first priority since its approach had been detected first.

In large cities, existing apparatus continued to be provided with safety shields to protect firefighters. Baltimore adopted "polycarbonate plastic material to protect its men and equipment. The $65,000 project equipped all fire apparatus with safety shields. Need for the added safety gathered momentum when Baltimore police had to rescue an entire fire company. All the firefighters required hospital treatment."[1] False alarms from alarm boxes turned into a problem without control. By 1978, FDNY was receiving more than 800 false alarms per day.[2] New alarm boxes required the person activating the alarm to speak to an emergency operator. Some new apparatus delivered to FDNY had enclosed cabs with locks on the doors. This was to prevent the apparatus from being stolen while the crew was occupied, such as inside a high-rise building.

This was the decade when light-colored apparatus came into use. It had been determined that red was one of the most difficult colors to detect at night. White was the easiest but white was difficult to spot under hazy or cloudy conditions. Hence, lime yellow and similar shades were adopted, and they adorned many new fire engines and trucks. Ward LaFrance is the apparatus builder most closely associated with the introduction of this color. In 1973, Pierce reported that 15 percent of its sales were for lime yellow, while Mack reported only five percent.[3] The new colors, despite their advantage, were never especially popular with either firefighters or fire buffs. Lime green also showed up as the color of adhesive strips attached to turnout gear, making firefighters more visible at night.

In the 1970s, FDNY experienced many milestones with regard to equipment. In 1972, it received 46 Mack pumpers and, for the first time in New York City, all pumpers were of the same make. Secondly, one of these 46 Macks was FDNY's 1,000th motorized pumper to be acquired. In 1973, FDNY retired its last wooden aerial from first-line service. In 1975, the last piece of gasoline-powered apparatus was retired from first-

---

[1] *The American City* (December 1971), p. 10.

[2] *Firehouse* (May 1979), p. 35.

[3] *The American City* (December 1972), pp. 78-79.

line service; all large first-line rigs were now diesel-powered. In the mid-1970s, there were severe budget cuts that reduced the number of firefighters and brought new equipment acquisitions to a virtual halt. Late in the decade, some funds were restored and, in 1980, American-LaFrance delivered 80 new pumpers.

The New York Fire Patrol bought some 1973 GMCs, and mounted on them fully enclosed bodies built by Independent Truck Co. In 1973, Los Angeles converted one of its 1948 Mack salvage wagons into a truck that carried and serviced air bottles carried by firefighters.

In 1974, the movie *The Towering Inferno* was released, starring Steve McQueen and Paul Newman. Both San Francisco's Fire Department and its Bank of America skyscraper had roles in the film, as did some fire apparatus from Los Angeles. The film dealt with a fire in a high-rise building. Cause of that blaze was overheated wiring that complied with the city's codes but which was less than the architect had specified.

The size of crews assigned to apparatus declined as firefighters' salaries went up and work hours went down. Smaller apparatus, mounted on mid-size commercial truck chassis, became more popular in large departments. Usually they carried two-man crews and were known as "attack" apparatus. They would reach the fire first, ahead of conventional engine and ladder companies. Labor was by now the most expensive item in a department's budget, so this practice resulted in the least initial response time since a city could operate attack apparatus with smaller crews. Orange, California, used a two-man flying squad to supplement other crews on calls throughout the city. Ambulances were upgraded and personnel required more training. Using radio links to emergency rooms, the attendants in the vehicle could practice various lifesaving measures.

More and more departments supplied their firefighters with self-contained breathing apparatus to be used inside burning structures. Boston ordered the use of masks at all structure fires, and smoke inhalation incidents involving Boston's firefighters dropped to one-fourth of their previous level.[4] Hose was made of lighter weight, but stronger materials as were its couplings and nozzles. Various foams and "slick" water also came into use, allowing smaller hose lines to be used. Garments and helmets were also made of lighter weight material, and some helmets could carry small radio receivers.

Computer programs became available to deal with station "location" problems. Applied to San Bernardino, for example:

> The city was broken up into 196 fire demand zones and the fire department figured there were between 40 and 50 sites where fire stations could be built. By manipulating the data to determine what arrangement of stations would yield a maximum response time, the program shows the fewest number of stations and sites. Then, the desired number of stations and the desired response time are balanced against each other to come out with the optimum, but still affordable, design.[5]

Detroit took delivery of a new fireboat in 1979. Fireboats were declining in popularity because of their crew costs. This was overcome by using smaller fireboats that made more use of hydraulics to control pipes and nozzles. Smaller fireboats could also operate in marinas, often the site of boat fires.

This would be a good year for many apparatus builders because federal programs of revenue sharing made funds available for use by municipalities. For a few brief years. cities didn't feel as strapped for funds and one part of this new-found wealth went for fire engines and trucks.

During this decade. American-LaFrance's parent company bought the Snorkel Fire Equipment Co. of St. Louis, the builder of elevating towers. In 1972, American-LaFrance introduced its "Pacemaker" series, and priced it between the "1000" and "Pioneer" models.

In 1973, American-LaFrance introduced its "Century" series, with "Century" applying to the 100th anniversary of the International Association of Fire Chiefs. One of the features of the American-LaFrance "Century" 100-foot aerial was a telescoping waterway that could deliver 1,000 gpm at the top of the extended foot-ladder. In 1975, the firm introduced a mini-pumper known as a "Stinger" attack pumper on a Dodge 4X4 chassis.

Beck fire apparatus were built in Cloverdale, California. Its first delivery was a brush rig.

Curtis-Heiser made its final fire apparatus deliveries in 1980, although both firms survive to this day.

---

[4] *Firehouse* (July 1980), p. 57.

[5] *The American City & County* (May 1978), p. 31.

Emergency One, one of the nation's leading apparatus builders today, was founded in Ocala, Florida, in 1974 by Bob Wormser, a retired playground equipment builder. The firm emphasized use of aluminum, which meant it could use lighter chassis, including commercial chassis. In the early days it kept in inventory Ford, GMC, Hendrickson, and Penfab chassis as well as Hale pumps of various sizes. This allowed the firm to guarantee delivery of an outfitted commercial chassis within 60 days. Emergency One also began building its own chassis, available in two models, the "Cyclone" and "Hurricane." Today the firm produces a complete range of apparatus styles and types.

FMC acquired Van Pelt, a well-known northern California apparatus builder, in 1978.

Mention was made previously of the Ford C, a cab-forward model introduced in 1957 that proved popular in the fire service. In a 1973 article, S.L. Menietti, the fire chief in Oakland, California, described how his department decided to buy new apparatus on commercial chassis, rather than custom makes. Money savings was the main reason; its two new Fords, fully outfitted, cost $35,500 each, compared with $55,000 for a custom make. They selected Ford C-800 chassis with a powertrain consisting of a Caterpillar 1600 diesel, a Spicer five-speed transmission, and a Rockwell rear axle. The powertrain selection took into account the city's many hills. The chassis were delivered to the fire department's shops where some wiring modifications were made to meet Oakland's requirements. Then the chassis were driven to a private shop that had delivered the lowest bid for installing pumps (a mid-ship pump driven off the transmission and a booster pump driven by the power takeoff), hose bed, cabinets, and pump controls. This period was also the beginning of the "fuel crisis," and Chief Menietti said this about diesel fuel:

> Diesel fuel, of course, is relatively non-volatile in comparison to gasoline. This is particularly important when fighting open fires, such as the hill fires in the Oakland area.
>
> Significantly lower fuel consumption of the diesels is not only a cost savings, but looms particularly important during the current fuel shortage. It also reduces the number of pieces of equipment necessary to contain a large fire.

The latter point was made dramatically at one fire scene where two trucks, one gasoline the other diesel, had worked side-by-side each pumping six lines at full capacity. The gasoline truck consumed a total of 87 gallons of fuel, which meant a tanker had to come to the scene to refuel it. The diesel used only 20 gallons and required no tanker.[6]

In the Foothill Fire Protection District in Southern California a GMC tanker/brush rig was built in the fire department's shops by paid firefighters. The vehicle was all-wheel drive and carried 1,500 gallons of water. All controls were inside the truck so it could operate while in motion. The rig took three months to build and went into service in 1980.

At about this time, General Safety Apparatus was being manufactured in North Branch, Minnesota. Most of it was sold to St. Paul and to other communities in Minnesota. It frequently used Waterous pumps.

Hahn continued in business, specializing in custom apparatus. Its tillered aerial ladders had enclosed tiller cabs with bulletproof windows (a sign of the times).

International Harvester, working with Howe, developed a custom cab-forward chassis for fire apparatus use. It had a five-man canopy cab. Howe's president, R.S. Howe, explained the relationship between the two companies:

> With custom fire trucks, manufacturers such as Howe are not large enough to maintain their own service organizations all over the country. That's why we like to work with a company such as International Harvester. They can provide this service through their 5,000 dealers and branches.[7]

In 1976, Howe was purchased by Grumman. Grumman introduced new apparatus lines named "Firecat," Wildcat," and "Minicat," all attempts to capitalize on the popular World War II Naval aircraft fighters that Grumman had built. Later, an "Attackcat" was introduced, intended for use either off-road or as an attack pumper. "Aerialcat" was the name given to Grumman's aerial platform models.

Ladder Towers Incorporated began in 1973 after Grove Manufacturing of Shady Grove, Pennsylvania, sold its aerial division. The new company initially supplied aerial ladders and aerial platforms to other chassis outfitters. Soon

---

[6] *The American City* (December 1979), p. 37.
[7] *A History of Howe, 1872-1972* (Anderson, Indiana, the company, 1972), p. 14.

it changed its name to LTI and began building complete apparatus.

Mack enjoyed many sales to major city departments for apparatus outfitted by itself or by others. Its chassis also carried specialized equipment such as wrecker/recovery vehicles and fuel tankers. Los Angeles County bought Mack tractors for pulling trailers with bulldozers for wildland fires. Two Mack chassis were intended for carrying fire apparatus. The model MC was a cab-forward version with a tilt cab available in sizes that could carry two, five, or seven firefighters. The Mack R was a conventional engine-forward model of fire chassis. Literature said to choose the chassis and then "have the body built and mounted by the body builder of your choice, to your own specifications, and to your own timetable, or specify a totally-built Mack pumper. When you order your Mack chassis, tell us the type of body and the builder, and we will prepare the chassis with components, fuel tank, lights and trim in the proper configuration. We will also provide detailed chassis specifications to help guide and expedite the job."

Mako Compressors, Inc. delivered to Miami an "air" truck, carried on a GMC chassis. It had a compressor and purifier, and stored air cylinders. At the rear was a platform where two cylinders could be refilled at the same time.

Maxim was a subsidiary of Seagrave during this decade and built both cab-forward and conventional (engine-forward) apparatus. The firm supplied aerial ladders to others.

During the decade, Pierce received a contract to build a fleet of rescue units for the U.S. Air Force. Its apparatus sales were growing and it was becoming the largest buyer of Waterous pumps. In 1973, Pierce entered into an agreement with LTI Ladder Co. to purchase aerial platforms. In 1975, Pierce received an order from Saudi Arabia for more than 700 units. Pierce used chassis supplied by Duplex, Hendrickson, and Oshkosh. It also used 4X4 chassis on Dodge, Chevrolet, and Ford chassis for its "Grass-hopper" brush rig. In 1979, the firm also acquired the rights to use the Pierce-Arrow name—a name associated with fine automobiles. (The firm displays a restored Pierce-Arrow car in the lobby of its main offices.) It also has named one of its apparatus lines the "Pierce-Arrow."

Pirsch continued to supply both custom and commercial chassis, and its ladders maintained the firm's good reputation. The fire trucks usually carried Hale pumps and were diesel-powered. Memphis was an especially loyal customer.

Seagrave, now part of FWD, made large deliveries to Baltimore, Chicago, Cincinnati, Los Angeles, New York, and Sacramento. The market began demanding 1,500-gpm pumps and, rather than reengineering the existing Seagrave model, the firm began purchasing pumps from Waterous, in South St. Paul. By the end of the decade about one-third of its deliveries were painted lime yellow.

Sutphen began expanding its markets and started making deliveries to a number of large cities, especially of ladder and aerial platform trucks. Similar to other manufacturers who were barely known, the firm was able to submit favorable bids and thus receive orders. Sutphen made deliveries to Boston, Cleveland, Detroit, and New York City.

In 1972, Ward LaFrance's founder, Adison Ward, died. In that same year, the firm introduced its command tower pumper, a pumper with an elevating tower that rose 23 feet to give the commander at the scene better visibility. During that same year, the firm made a concerted effort to penetrate West Coast markets and made large sales to San Francisco and Los Angeles. Ward LaFrance was one of the early suppliers of lime yellow apparatus. It also teamed with United States Steel Corp. to design an advance pumper, called the "Vantage." Despite all these efforts, the firm went out of business in 1979, and many of its assets were taken over by a successor firm, known as Ward 79.

Westates continued in operation, concentrating on Western markets. It built both custom and commercial models and continued to rely on Waterous pumps.

Western States Fire Apparatus was located in Cornelius, Oregon, and supplied mainly rural markets. However, it made occasional sales to large cities in the Pacific Northwest, such as Portland.

San Jose took delivery of this 1971 American-LaFrance Ladder Chief rear-mount 100-foot aerial. It ran as Truck 18. (Photo courtesy Wayne Sorensen)

San Jose operated this 1971 American-LaFrance 100-foot aerial. This was the first rear-mount 100-foot aerial in the department. The aerial ladder is no longer serviceable. The unit runs as a ladder truck. This unit was in service as Truck 2 and Truck 16. (Photo courtesy Wayne Sorensen)

Westates used a 1971 Chevrolet chassis to build this light truck for San Jose.

A 1971 Ford/Maxim hose wagon with a 50-foot Tele-Squrt, in-service as Engine 39 in Boston. (Photo courtesy Dick Adelman)

Pirsch built this 1971 100-foot aerial on a Ford C-9000 chassis for Cleveland. Tandem rear axles provided additional stability for the rear-mount aerial. (Photo courtesy Dick Adelman)

Paterson, New Jersey's Engine 8, a 1971 Hahn with a 1,250-gpm pump, two booster reels, and a deck gun. (Photo courtesy Dick Adelman)

St. Paul's Ladder 10 was this 100-foot aerial mounted by Thibault on a 1971 International chassis. Note the second cab. (Photo courtesy Dick Adelman)

Heavily loaded 1971 International Light Plant No. 2 in service in Boston. (Photo courtesy Dick Adelman)

Atlanta's Truck 30, a 1971 Pirsch with a 75-foot aerial carried on a straight frame. Rear compartment is labeled "Life Net." (Photo courtesy Dick Adelman)

Belmont, California, used this 1971 Seagrave Rear Admiral 100-foot aerial. Powertrain was a Detroit diesel engine and an Allison transmission. (Photo courtesy Wayne Sorensen)

Baltimore received five diesel-powered Seagrave 1,000-gpm triple combinations in 1971 with four-door sedan cabs. The roof was removable to get to the engine in event of major engine work. (Photo courtesy Dick Adelman)

Sunnyvale, California, used a 1956 Coast chassis to build this 1972 pumper. Mack R-Model sheet metal and cab were used on the front of the rig. It is diesel powered, and has a 1,000-gpm pump and 500-gallon booster tank. (Photo courtesy Wayne Sorensen)

Tucson, Arizona, purchased the first 150-foot elevating platform in 1972. This was the tallest aerial built and used in the United States. Sacramento then purchased this truck from Tucson, and it became Sacramento's second 150-foot Firebird. The platform was built on a Duplex chassis. It's shown with outriggers extended, and with all 10 wheels clear of the ground. (Photo courtesy Wayne Sorensen)

One of five Ford chassis with 1,250-gpm Hale pumps delivered to Oakland, California, from 1970 until 1973. Involved in the construction of the apparatus were L.N. Curtis & Sons, who produced the specifications and Earl Sherman & Co., who did much of the work. The Ford C had a tilt-cab, and was powered by a 225-hp Caterpillar diesel. The rigs had 300-gallon booster tanks with separate booster pumps. (Photo courtesy Earl Sherman & Co.)

Water is heavy and the quantity that a truck can carry is often limited by the truck's load-capacity. Mount Vernon, New Hampshire, operated this 1971 International with dual rear axles to carry a 2,800-gallon tank. Rack on side of tank holds a canvas fold-up tank that is placed on the ground at the fire site. The tanker discharges into it and leaves to find another load of water. The truck also carries a portable pump. (Photo courtesy Roland Boulet)

One of two Kenworth/L.N. Curtis 1,500-gpm triple combination pumpers that were delivered to Seattle in 1972. The rig had an enclosed cab, and 400-gallon booster tank with bodywork by Heiser. The powerplant was a 265-hp Detroit diesel engine. In 1988, the crew cab ceiling height was raised, and hard suctions and suction brackets replaced with breathing apparatus compartments. (Photo courtesy Bill Hattersley)

The Mack R Series was introduced as a replacement for the long running Mack B Series. The Mack R Series had the Maxidyne constant diesel power and Maxitorque transmission. Quakertown, Pennsylvania, ran this large 1972 rescue built by Saulsbury. (Photo courtesy Saulsbury Fire Equipment Co.)

Chicago purchased this Pirsch rear-mount aerial built on a 1972 Mack CF chassis. (Photo courtesy Bill Friedrich)

Barton-American used a 1972 Oshkosh chassis to build this massive unit for Pine Hills, Florida. It has a 1,000-gpm pump and a rear-mount 55-foot Aqua-Jet ladder. (Photo courtesy Dick Adelman)

Charlotte, North Carolina, bought this 1972 Pierce, built on a Hendrickson chassis. It carried a 1,000-gpm pump. (Photo courtesy Dick Adelman)

Working at a fire is a 1972 Seagrave 100-foot aerial used in San Francisco as Truck 6. The unit has a hydraulic ladder tower table leveling device, used when the truck is spotted on a hill. Tiller cab shown at rear is fixed in position. (Photo courtesy Thom Taggart)

A Ward LaFrance demonstrator with an elevating 22-foot command tower on a 1972 Ambassador custom chassis 1,250-gpm pump. (Photo courtesy Dick Adelman)

Ward LaFrance and United States Steel created this "Vantage" pumper design in 1972, intended for placement on commercial truck chassis. The pump was behind a roll-up door. (Photo courtesy Ward LaFrance)

Baltimore's Engine 14 was this 1973 American-LaFrance "Pacemaker" 1,000-gpm triple combination. (Photo courtesy Dick Adelman)

In 1995, San Jose spent $90,000 to refurbish this 1973 American-LaFrance Pacemaker, shown in-service here as Engine 28. The color was changed from lime green to red. The engine has a 1,500-gpm pump and a 500-gallon water tank. (Photo courtesy Wayne Sorensen)

A 1973 C-tilt-cab Ford/Maynard used as hose wagon 10 in Boston, Massachusetts. The wagon has two fixed turret pipes. (Photo courtesy Dick Adelman)

This 1973 Ford/Hahn 1,000-gpm pumper was run by Leipsic, Delaware. It carried 1,000 gallons of water. (Photo courtesy Dick Adelman)

Engine 7 in Sacramento used this 1973 Ford-Howe with a 1,250-gpm pump and 500-gallon booster tank. Pump controls are top mounted. (Photo courtesy Wayne Sorensen)

In 1973, Howe Fire Apparatus Co. of Anderson, Indiana, used a Hendrickson six-wheel chassis to build a 1,000-gpm Quint for Wayne Township, Indiana. It has a 100-foot aerial and a 300-gallon booster tank. (Photo courtesy Dick Adelman)

A 1973 International Loadstar 1700 with bodywork by Westates used by Light Unit 13, second section of Truck 13 in San Jose. It was equipped with a 35-foot light boom and 12.5-kw power generator. (Photo courtesy Wayne Sorensen)

A 1973 International chassis outfitted by Westates to make a light truck for San Jose. The unit has a 12.5-kw generator and a 35-foot light tower that is shown extended. In San Jose, light trucks ran as second units to ladder companies.

A 1973 Kenworth chassis with a Detroit diesel was used by L.N. Curtis and the Heiser Body Co. to build this ladder truck for Seattle. This was one of an order of five. The 100-foot aerial ladders were from Maxim. (Photo courtesy Bill Hattersley)

Shelbyville, Tennessee, purchased this impressive 75-foot Pitman Snorkel mounted on an Oshkosh chassis, with body-work by Pierce, in 1973. (Photo courtesy Dick Adelman)

Atlanta ran this 1973 Pirsch built on a Hendrickson chassis. It had a 1,000-gpm pump and a 55-foot Tele-Squrt tower. (Photo courtesy Dick Adelman)

Washington-Perry Township, near Dublin, Ohio, bought this 1973 Sutphen custom 1,250-gpm triple combination. (Photo courtesy Wayne Sorensen)

Cambridge, Ohio, ran this Sutphen triple combination in 1973. The 1,250-gpm triple came with a canopy cab. (Photo courtesy Wayne Sorensen)

In 1973, Ward LaFrance delivered this 75-foot Hi-Ranger elevating platform to the Dallas-Fort Worth Airport. The platform is mounted on a low-profile cab to reduce height. Note the outrigger jacks for stability. (Photo courtesy Dick Adelman)

Grafton, Vermont, operated this unusual all-wheel-drive 1973 Ward LaFrance 1,500-gpm pumper with an 50-foot Tele-Squrt. (Photo courtesy Roland Boulet)

Shaker Heights, Ohio's Engine 2, a 1974 American-LaFrance 1,250-gpm pumper with a 55-foot Tele-Squrt provides mutual aid to a nearby community. The firefighter climbing the boom wears turnout gear, a fiberglass helmet with faceshield, plus a mask connected with backpack breathing apparatus. (Photo courtesy John McCown and John Sytsma)

FTI used a 1974 Dodge heavy-duty chassis to build Engine 3 for Hamtramck, Michigan. It has a 1,000-gpm pump with control panel under rear seat of the crew cab. Dodge dropped out of the heavy truck market in the mid-1970s.

San Francisco bought three of these "attack" hose wagons from Crown in 1974. They each carry 2,000 feet of three-inch hose plus a 55-foot Tele-Squrt, shown here partially extended and with the outrigger jacks extended. This is Tender 7. Power comes from a 225-hp Caterpillar diesel. (Photo courtesy Wayne Sorensen)

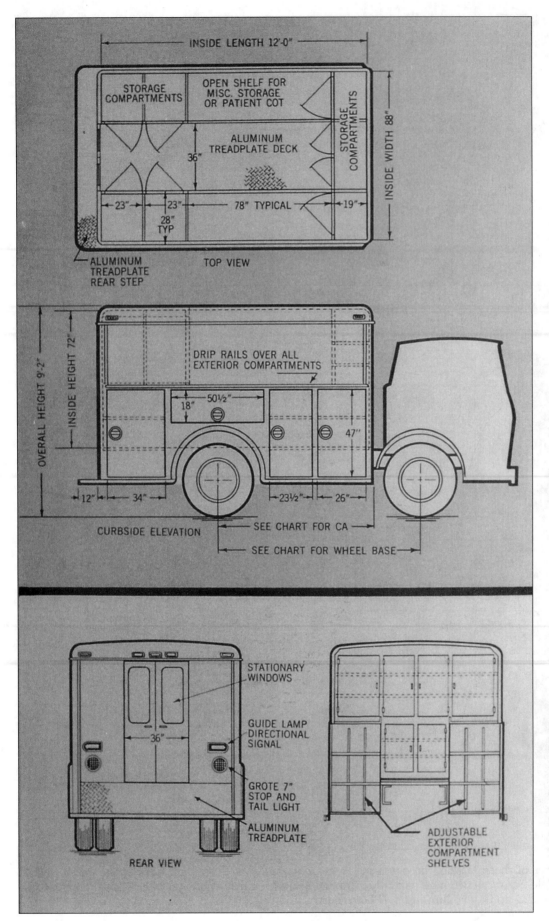

INSIDE LENGTH 12'-0"

STORAGE COMPARTMENTS

OPEN SHELF FOR MISC. STORAGE OR PATIENT COT

STORAGE COMPARTMENTS

ALUMINUM TREADPLATE DECK

36"

INSIDE WIDTH 88"

23" 23" 78" TYPICAL 19"

28" TYP

ALUMINUM TREADPLATE REAR STEP

TOP VIEW

OVERALL HEIGHT 9'-2"

INSIDE HEIGHT 72"

DRIP RAILS OVER ALL EXTERIOR COMPARTMENTS

18" 50½"

47"

12" 34" 23½" 26"

CURBSIDE ELEVATION

SEE CHART FOR CA

SEE CHART FOR WHEEL BASE

STATIONARY WINDOWS

GUIDE LAMP DIRECTIONAL SIGNAL

36"

GROTE 7" STOP AND TAIL LIGHT

ALUMINUM TREADPLATE

REAR VIEW

ADJUSTABLE EXTERIOR COMPARTMENT SHELVES

 74ger

Drawing from some Gerstenslager literature from the 1970s showing a 12-foot enclosed rescue body intended to fit on Ford C tilt-cab chassis. The body contained mainly equipment cabinets, although it could accommodate a cot. (Photo courtesy Gerstenslager)

Sutphen built a triple combination pumper on the 1974 Ford C cab tilt-cab chassis. Washington, D.C.'s Engine 27 had a 750-gpm pump, 250-gallon booster tank and a crew module in back of the cab. (Photo courtesy Roland Boulet)

A 1974 Hendrickson chassis with a mounted 135-foot Morita-lift, which was Japanese-made. Bodywork was done by Pierce. There was a two-man elevator through the center of the extended six-section aerial ladder. The truck served as Ladder 2 in Chicago, then as Ladder 1. (Photo courtesy Dick Adelman)

Howe built a number of aerial trucks. Turtle Creek, Pennsylvania's Truck 1 had a 100-foot mid-mount Grove aerial mounted on a 1974 Hendrickson tandem rear axle chassis. This large truck has a five-man canopy cab. (Photo courtesy Dick Adelman)

Chicago used this 1974 Mack MB series as a fuel wagon. (Photo courtesy Dick Adelman)

Emergency One rebuilt this 1974 Mack/Howe pumper for Chicago. The pump is rated at 1,250 gpm, and there's a 500-gallon booster tank. (Photo courtesy Bill Friedrich)

Gerstenslager Corp. of Wooster, Ohio, used a 1974 Mack chassis to build a command vehicle for Phoenix, Arizona. (Photo courtesy Bill Hattersley)

The Howe Fire Apparatus Co. delivered ten 1,250-gpm triple combinations on Mack MB chassis for Chicago. The pumpers were powered by a six-cylinder Maxidyne ENT 675 diesel engine. (Photo courtesy Dick Adelman)

The Centerville-Osterville Fire District, in Massachusetts, operated this 1974 Maxim brush breaker for fighting fires in wildlands. The tandem rear axle apparatus had a 500-gpm pump and 800-gallon water tank. (Photo courtesy Dick Adelman)

In 1974, Oren-Roanoke, a subsidiary of Howe Fire Apparatus Co., built this 2,000-gpm pumper for Ocean City, Maryland. A Duplex chassis was employed and a Cincinnati canopy cab encloses this driver and crew. (Photo courtesy Dick Adelman)

Oren-Roanoke built this ladder truck on a 1974 Hendrickson chassis for Haggerstown, Maryland. The rear-mount ladder is a 100-foot Grove. Note tall equipment lockers at mid-ship. (Photo courtesy Dick Adelman)

Pierce used this 1974 Hendrickson chassis to build Syracuse's Engine 8. The pumper is equipped with a 2,000-gpm pump and a 50-foot Hi-stream Ladder. (Photo courtesy Dick Adelman)

A 1974 Hendrickson chassis was used by Pirsch to build a massive 1,000-gpm triple combination for Opelika, Alabama. (Photo courtesy Pirsch-Dick Adelman)

Louisville purchased this 1974 1,000-gpm Pirsch pumper with a 55-foot Tele-Squrt. The unit has the Pirsch custom cab and chassis. (Photo courtesy Dick Adelman)

Chicago's 1974 Seagrave with a rear-mounted aerial. Seagrave first used this configuration on its water towers. Truck 7 was rebuilt by Seagrave in 1992 and returned to service as Truck 22. (Photo courtesy Bill Friedrich)

This 1974 Seagrave tractor-drawn 100-foot aerial in service as Truck 3 in Chattanooga. Note the open tiller position. (Photo courtesy Dick Adelman)

Syracuse purchased this 1974 Sutphen 85-foot aerial tower, with a 1,000-gpm pump. (Photo courtesy Dick Adelman)

A 1975 American-LaFrance Pioneer II, the successor to Pioneer I. Pioneer II is a custom pumper with features of the 1000 series. The mid-ship mounted pump is the American-LaFrance Twinflow, two-stage, parallel series fire pump. Shown is Santa Clara's Engine 8 equipped with a 1,250-gpm pump, a 500-gallon booster tank, and a Detroit diesel engine. (Photo courtesy Wayne Sorensen)

The Bureau of Equipment, San Francisco Fire Department operates this 1975 heavy-duty tow truck. It has a Ford L chassis with a mounted 25-ton Holmes hoist. The truck is powered by a Detroit diesel, 350-hp engine. (Photo courtesy Wayne Sorensen).

In 1975, FWD delivered five pumpers to San Jose. They were equipped with 1,500-gpm pumps and had 500-gallon booster tanks. Shown is Engine 6. (Photo courtesy Wayne Sorensen)

Western States built this interesting 1,250-gpm front-mounted pumper on an imposing 1975 FWD chassis equipped pump and 1,500-gallon booster tank. Rig is operated in Umatilla, Oregon. (Photo courtesy Bill Hattersley)

The New Jersey Fire Equipment Co. sold Oren apparatus under the name of Great Eastern in its territory. This 1,250-gpm custom triple combination on a duplex semi-cab chassis was made for New Brunswick, New Jersey. (Photo courtesy The New Jersey Fire Equipment Co.)

A 1975 Hendrickson-Firebird, 90-foot Calavar platform ladder used as Truck 8 in Sacramento. It was powered by a 8V-71 diesel engine. (Photo courtesy Wayne Sorensen)

Chicago purchased this 1975 Mack MB tractor for hauling older FWD ladder trailers to Clintonville, Wisconsin, where they were to be rebuilt and have new Seagrave ladders installed. Later, the Mack was outfitted with two large Stang guns and the unit was operated as a turret wagon. (Photo courtesy Bill Friedrich)

The San Jose Fire Department accepted two 1975 Oshkosh M-1500 crash trucks for use at the airport. They were equipped with 1,000-gpm pumps, 1,500-gallon water tanks and had 180 gallons of foam concentrate. Shown is crash 2A demonstrating its roof turret. (Photo courtesy Wayne Sorensen)

A 1975 Seagrave P cab 1,500-gpm triple combination operated by Chicago as Engine 7. It has a 500-gallon water tank. (Photo courtesy Bill Friedrich)

A 1976 Chevrolet chassis used by Chicago to mount smoke ejector No. 2. (Photo courtesy Bill Friedrich)

In 1976, American-LaFrance delivered 20 Detroit diesel-powered 1,000-gpm triple combination pumpers to Memphis. This is Engine 36, parked. (Photo courtesy Wayne Sorensen)

Engine 36 pumping at oil refinery drill. It's shown taking water from the hydrant through its front suction intake. Notice all the lines coming off the engine. (Photo courtesy Wayne Sorensen)

Sweet Home, Oregon, used this 2,000-gallon tanker from Western States. It's mounted on a three-axle 1976 Ford L chassis, and carries a 1,250-gpm front-mount pump. (Photo courtesy Bill Hattersley)

In 1975, Sacramento purchased two Firebird elevating platforms. One was a 90-foot unit and the other a 150-foot unit. Both were on Hendrickson chassis powered by Detroit diesels. Shown is Truck 8's 90-foot tower. (Photo courtesy Wayne Sorensen)

Seattle's Engine 20, a huge 1976 Kenworth/Curtis triple combination 1,750-gpm pumper. Heiser, of Seattle, did the final bodywork. The truck has a 400-gallon booster tank. (Photo courtesy Bill Hattersley)

A 1976 Mack Series MB 1,000-gpm pumper that ran as Engine 67 in Kansas City, Missouri. These flat-faced rigs were short and maneuverable in close quarters. (Photo courtesy Dick Adelman)

A 1976 Mack/Gerstenslager converted to a "scene rehabilitation unit" from a heavy rescue truck by the Phoenix Fire Department. The unit is used to "cool down" and check firefighters working at large fires. This is a critical problem in Phoenix because of the hot weather. (Photo courtesy Bill Hattersley)

One of two 1976 Mack MB Series chassis used by Howe to build 1,250-gpm triple combinations for Indianapolis. Pump controls are "top mounted" on step behind cab, looking rearward. (Photo courtesy Bill Friedrich)

In 1990, Pierce rebuilt Cheshire, Connecticut's 1976 Maxim rescue squad. (Photo courtesy Dick Adelman)

Syracuse purchased this 1976 Pierce 2,000-gpm pumper mounted on a Hendrickson chassis. Visible at the top is a 50-foot Histream ladder. (Photo courtesy Dick Adelman)

Pierce delivered to Brigham City, Utah, this 1976 Ford Model F minipumper with a 300-gpm pump and 250-gallon booster tank. (Photo courtesy Bill Hattersley)

Boston ran this 1976 Seagrave 100-foot aerial as Ladder 10. The truck has a four-door sedan cab, enclosed ladder beds, and the tillerman's cab was enclosed. (Photo courtesy Dick Adelman)

Van Pelt used a 1976 Duplex chassis to build a 1,250-gpm custom pumper for Santa Cruz, California. Powered by a Detroit diesel, the unit carries 1,000 gallons of water. (Photo courtesy Wayne Sorensen)

Two big hose reels are carried on this 1976 Ward LaFrance 1,250-gpm pumper that was converted into a hose wagon by the Meadowwood County Area Fire Department in Fitzwillian, New Hampshire. The reels carry 6,000 feet of four-inch hose. (Photo courtesy Roland Boulet)

Chicago's Engine 34 ran this 1977 American-LaFrance Century 1,500-gpm triple combination pumper. (Photo courtesy Dick Adelman)

Shown at work on a mutual aid call is East Cleveland, Ohio's 1977 American-LaFrance "Century" quintuple. It has a 1,500-gpm pump and a 100-foot aerial. (Photo courtesy John Sytsma)

Chicago's Engine 46 was this 1977 American-LaFrance 2,000-gpm pumper. Soft suction hose is carried behind the front bumper. Note Dalmatian above pump panel. (Photo courtesy Bill Friedrich)

A 1976-77 Ford chassis used by Ansul to build a combination pumper and dry chemical unit. Foam can extinguish some fires three to five times faster than water.

San Jose ran two-piece truck companies, with the second unit being a light wagon. Light Unit 4 is on a 1977 International chassis that has been outfitted by Westates. The truck is powered by a Detroit 8V-71 diesel engine. It carries a 35-foot light tower, a 20-kw generator, and salvage covers.

A 1977 International Paystar used by Welch to build tanker 2 for San Jose. It's equipped with a 250-gpm pump and 2,500-gallon water tank. Dual rear axles are needed to carry load. Powerplant is a Cummins diesel engine. (Photo courtesy Wayne Sorensen)

Worcester purchased this 1977 Maxim custom pumper with a 1,250-gpm pump, plus a 500-gallon booster tank. (Photo courtesy Ray Stevens)

Santa Fe, New Mexico, ran this 2,000-gallon tanker outfitted by 3-D on a 1978 Chevrolet chassis. (Photo courtesy Bill Hattersley)

The first Crown Firecoach built, Model CP 195-93, a 1,250-gpm triple combination with a 300-gallon water tank. This Crown demonstrator was sold to West Covina, California. CREDIT: Larry Arnold

Sultan, Washington, bought this 1958 Diamond-T/Howard Cooper triple combination. It had a 500-gpm pump and carried 1,000 gallons of water. CREDIT: Bill Hattersley

Seattle's 1960 "900" Series American-LaFrance tractor-trailer with 100-foot metal, hydraulically-operated, four-section aerial ladder was delivered in 1961 with an Allison-Boeing gasoline turbine 325-hp experimental engine. It was returned to American-LaFrance and delivered back to Seattle in 1962 with a new 323-hp Hall-Scott engine and a Fuller standard transmission. Tiller cab was enclosed in 1977 and a new 350-hp Detroit diesel engine and Allison automatic transmission were provided. It was in service as Ladders 1 and 4. CREDIT: Bill Hattersley

A 1964 Brockway/Seagrave used in Bowie, Maryland. It's diesel-powered. CREDIT: Ray Stevens

A 1964 Pirsch cab-forward model with a flat, plain front view. The rig has a 1,250-gpm pump with a 500-gallon booster tank. Acquired through annexation by the Portland (Oregon) Fire Department. Running as Reserve Engine 124, and painted school bus yellow and cream.
CREDIT:
Bill Hattersley.

Western States Fire Apparatus used a 1967 Ford C chassis to build this pumper for the Santa Clara Fire Protection District. It had an American 1,250-gpm pump and a 600-gallon booster tank. CREDIT: Western States Fire Apparatus

This is a 1967 Young Crusader 1,000-gpm triple combination built for Chincoteque, Virginia. The pumper has a top mount pump control panel. The operator can look in all directions, and is protected from street traffic. Note the flashers integrated into the front corners of the cab roof.
CREDIT: Ray Stevens

Cheltenham, Pennsylvania, used this 1971 Mack CF Aerialscope. Note the ladder on top of boom. Stabilizing jacks and outriggers are in place.
CREDIT: Mack

Seattle's 1969 Kenworth/Maxim Truck 10. The trailer was pulled by a Kenworth tractor, powered by a Detroit diesel, 350-hp engine. The Maxim four-section, metal 100-foot aerial was hydraulically operated.
CREDIT: Bill Hattersley

Chicago's Truck 31 was this 1973 American-LaFrance 100-foot, rear-mount aerial. CREDIT: Bill Friedrich

A 1973 Walter/Yankee airport crash-rescue unit used in Pocatello, Idaho. It carries a 350-gpm pump, 1,000 gallons of water, and a foam unit.

Vancouver, British Columbia, Canada, purchased this 125-foot Calavar Firebird elevating platform in 1976. The tower was on a 10-wheel Hendrickson chassis. This was the first elevating platform in Canada and the fourth one built by Calavar. The tower had a vertical reach of 125 feet and a horizontal reach of 66 feet. The unit cost $165,000 at that time. CREDIT: Bill Hattersley

Odessa, Delaware, operates this 1979 Freightliner salvage and rescue truck. Note the heavy-duty winch in front. CREDIT: Ray Stevens

A 1981 Ford/Westates, with a 1,500-gpm pump and 500-gallon water tank, used by Oakland, California. CREDIT: Westates

Lawrence Livermore Laboratory in Northern California uses this 1982 Emergency One 110-foot rear-mount aerial ladder truck. A Hendrickson chassis was used to build the rig, which carries a 1,500-gpm pump, a 200-gallon booster tank, a 30-gallon foam tank, and a separate generator.
CREDIT:
Emergency One

A 1982 Seagrave six-wheel chassis was used to mount an 85-foot snorkel, with a 1,500-gpm pump and bodywork by Pierce. It ran as Chicago's Snorkel 1. CREDIT: Bill Friedrich

A mid-1980s Oshkosh T-3000 airport crash truck used in Fairbanks, Alaska. It has an 1,800-gpm pump, and carries 3,000 gallons of water plus 405 gallons of foam.
CREDIT: Oshkosh Truck Corp.

This large unit ran as Truck 1 in Sunnyvale, California. It was a 1986 Grumman quint carrying a 1,500-gpm pump, 300 gallons of water, and a 102-foot tower ladder. CREDIT: Bill Hattersley

A 1989 Olympian tractor with a 106-foot LTI ladder in service as Truck 6 in Portland, Oregon. CREDIT: Bill Hattersley

Everett, Washington, purchased this 1990 Emergency One 1,500-gpm pumper. It's built on Emergency One's "Hurricane" chassis and carries a 500-gallon booster tank. It runs as Engine 2.
CREDIT: Bill Hattersley

Los Angeles uses this 1992 Simon Duplex with a 100-foot Simon-LTI aerial ladder. The truck carries an additional 264 feet of ground ladders. The rig is powered by a Cummins diesel. Horizontal white stripe makes truck more visible at night. CREDIT: Simon-LTI

In the early-1990s, Towers Fire Apparatus Co., of Freeburg, Illinois, built this pumper with a Tele-Squrt elevating tower for Scottsburg, Indiana.
CREDIT: Towers Fire Apparatus Co.

Indianapolis bought this Simon Duplex in 1993. Its Simon-LTI tower can carry a payload of 750 pounds, and handle a water flow of 1,000 gpm. Flashing light bars above cab are parallel to the side of the truck.
CREDIT: Simon-LTI

A 1995 Oshkosh T-series airport crash truck equipped with a "snozzle." The snozzle is on an articulated boom that can be raised to 50 feet in the air, nearly straight above the truck, or be lowered to the ground, about 20 feet in front of the truck. It is equipped with a piercing nozzle that can penetrate the airplane's fuselage. A video camera with a zoom lens can also be placed on the boom tip, which will transmit the picture back to the truck's cab so the operator will know what action to take.
CREDIT: Oshkosh Truck Corp.

Ward LaFrance Presidential Series (custom).

Diplomat Aerial
Ladder Size: 65, 75, 85, 100 Ft.

Courier Brush Truck
Pump Size: 150, 200, 300 G.P.M.

Senator Snorkel
Working Height: 65, 75, 80, 85 Ft.

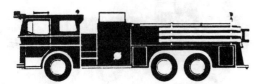

Envoy Tanker
Tank Size: 1000, 1250, 1500, 2000 Gal.

Statesman Aircraft — Fire Rescue
Tank Size: 1000, 1500, 2000, 2500, 3000, 3500, 4000 Gal.

Delegate Rescue

77war

Governor Foam
Tank Size: 500, 750, 1000, 1200 Gal.

Ambassador Pumper
Pump Size: 500, 750, 1000, 1250, 1500, 1750, 2000 G.P.M.

Congressman Light Truck
Generator Size: 5000, 10000, 15000 Watts

"Custom" apparatus manufacturers also outfit chassis of commercial makes of trucks. Here are the custom and commercial models offered by Ward LaFrance in the late-1970s. (Photo courtesy Ward LaFrance)

Ward LaFrance Constellation Series (commercial).

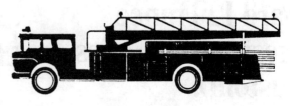

Venus Aerial
Ladder Size: 65, 75, 85, 100 Ft.

Mercury Brush Truck
Pump Size: 150, 200, 300 G.P.M.

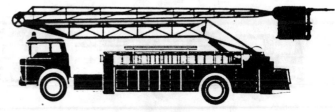

Apollo Snorkel
Working Height: 65, 75, 80, 85 Ft.

Neptune Tanker
Tank Size: 1000, 1250, 1500, 2000 Gal.

Saturn Aircraft — Fire Rescue
Tank Size: 1000, 1500, 2000, 2500, 3000, 3500, 4000 Gal.

Gemini Rescue

Aurora Foam
Tank Size: 500, 750, 1000, 1250 Gal.

Comet Pumper
Pump Size: 500, 750, 1000, 1250 G.P.M.

Star Light Truck
Generator Size: 5000, 10000, 15000 Watts

Jarrettsville, Maryland, ran this 1978 FMC custom pumper that had a 1,500-gpm pump and a 500-gallon booster tank. Transverse hose beds carry smaller hose. (Photo courtesy Ray Stevens)

A 1978 Ford 600 C tilt-cab used by fire department shops to build Hose Wagon 1 in Sacramento. Unit has a fixed turret pipe. (Photo courtesy Wayne Sorensen)

Emergency One used this 1978 Ford C chassis to build a 1,000-gpm pumper for Salt Lake City. A Hale pump was installed, along with a 500-gallon booster tank. It's shown at a working fire with the tilt-cab raised to increase cooling for the engine. (Photo courtesy John Sytsma)

One of Trenton, New Jersey's 1978 FTIs, with a 1,000-gpm pump and 500-gallon tank. (Photo courtesy Ray Stevens)

Welch Fire Equipment, of Marion, Wisconsin, used a 1978 International Cargostar 1610 to build Sacramento's Hose Tender 5. (Photo courtesy Wayne Sorensen)

A 1978 International Cargostar 1610B chassis used by Welch to build Compressor 12 for Sacramento. (Photo courtesy Wayne Sorensen)

The Memphis Fire Department used this airport crash truck mounted on a 1978 Oshkosh P-15 chassis. It carried 6,000 gallons of water, foam equipment, and a 2,400-gpm turret. (Photo courtesy Wayne Sorensen)

Rear view shows open tiller seat on San Francisco's Truck 3, a 1978 Seagrave, tractor-drawn, 100-foot aerial. The ladder bed is filled with wooden ladders, preferred by the San Francisco Fire Department because of the overhead wires used by the city's transit system. Also visible is the compartment for a high-speed rescue saw. In the rear is a 1985 Kenworth pumper. Fire site was San Francisco's Hilton Hotel. (Photo courtesy Thom Taggart)

A 1978 Seagrave low cab tractor with a large glass rear window. The powerplant is a 350-hp Detroit diesel V-8 engine. The tractor is pulling a 100-foot aerial trailer and is in-service as Truck 17, San Francisco. (Photo courtesy Wayne Sorensen)

One of two 1978 Westates 1,500-gpm pumpers on San Jose's roster. They were built on Penfab chassis. The booster tank carries 1,000 gallons and the powerplant is a Detroit diesel. (Photo courtesy Wayne Sorensen)

A 1979 American-LaFrance 55-foot snorkel powered by a Detroit diesel engine that ran in Memphis as Snorkel Squad 2. (Photo courtesy Wayne Sorensen)

Hockessin, Delaware, used a Hamerly rescue body on a 1979 Autocar chassis. (Photo courtesy Dick Adelman)

Oakland, California, operates many Westates pumpers. Engine 28 is mounted on a 1979 Ford Louisville chassis, and is equipped with a 1,500-gpm pump and a 500-gallon booster tank. The truck's power is a V-6 diesel. (Photo courtesy Wayne Sorensen)

A 1979 Great Eastern custom 1,500-gpm pumper used by East Rutherford, New Jersey. It ran as Engine 3. Note boot rack above suction hose. (Photo courtesy Ernest N. Day)

In 1979, Hahn built this 106-foot "Fire Spire" for Harrisonburg, Virginia. Hydraulic jacks stabilize the rig when the aerial is lifted. (Photo courtesy Dick Adelman)

This 1979 Maxim 100-foot rear-mounted aerial on a three-axle chassis was in service at Elmont, New York. (Photo courtesy Dick Adelman)

Santa Clara purchased two 1979 Seagrave Models WB-24068. Shown is Engine 1 with a 1,250-gpm pump and 500-gallon booster tank. (Photo courtesy Wayne Sorensen)

One of two 1979 Seagrave "W" cab 1,500-gpm pumpers equipped with 500-gallon booster tanks. Note the large glass side window. Shown is Engine 1 of Santa Clara. (Photo courtesy Wayne Sorensen)

The Seagrave PC20068 was a popular chassis used by Western States. This is Tualatin, Oregon's 1979 triple combination with a Barton American front mounted 1,250-gpm pump. The unit's power was a Detroit diesel 8V-71 engine. (Photo courtesy Bill Hattersley)

Saratoga, California, rebuilt its 1979 Seagrave "P" cab 1,500-gpm pumper equipped with a 500-gallon booster tank. The unit is powered by a Detroit 8V-71 diesel engine. (Photo courtesy Wayne Sorensen)

The Camden-Wyoming Fire Department in Delaware ran this large 1980 American-LaFrance Century with an 85-foot Pitman Snorkel. (Photo courtesy Dick Adelman)

Nashville's Snorkel 1 was an 85-foot Pitman elevated platform carried on a 1980 American-LaFrance chassis. (Photo courtesy Dick Adelman)

A 1980 Crown Firecoach in-service at Roseville, California, equipped with a 1,500-gpm pump, 500-gallon water tank and 50-foot Tele-Squrt. The unit is powered by a Detroit diesel engine. (Photo courtesy Wayne Sorensen)

East Dover, New Jersey, used a 1980 Dodge D chassis for a hose tender. It carries 4,000 feet of five-inch hose. (Photo courtesy Ray Stevens)

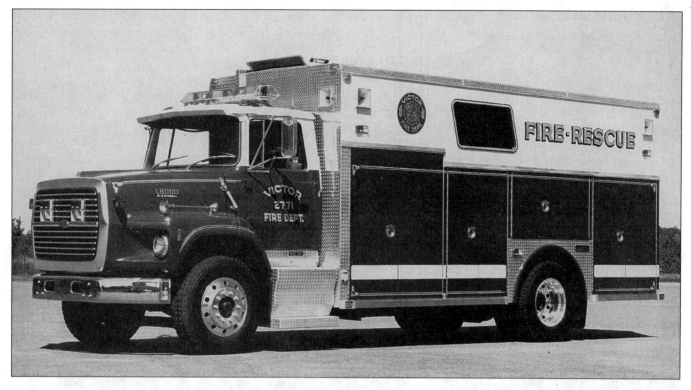

Circa-1980 Ford/Saulsbury rescue unit ran in Victor, New York. Note how warning lights have been placed in the grille. The L-8000 Ford is diesel-powered. (Photo courtesy Saulsbury)

This 1980 International S-Series six-wheel tractor was used by Clark County, Nevada, departmental shops to build Crash 44. It has a large mounted turret pipe, a 750-gpm pump and a large tandem-axle trailer containing 5,000 gallons of water and 500 gallons of AFFF. (Photo courtesy Bill Friedrich)

4-Guys, Incorporated of Meyersdale, Pennsylvania, used a Mack 1980 three-axle chassis to build this huge 3,000-gallon tanker with a 1,000-gpm front-mount pump for Rainview Township, Pennsylvania. (Photo courtesy Dick Adelman)

A 1980 Mack CF with a 75-foot Aerialscope, operated by Salt Lake County, Utah. (Photo courtesy John F. Sytsma)

Salt Lake County's 1980 Mack Aerialscope at a mutual aid fire in Murray, Utah, in 1994. Aerialscope is shown with jacks in place and 2,000 gpm of water flowing from the bucket. It knocked the fire down in less than five minutes. (Photo courtesy John F. Sytsma)

Seattle's Engine 37, one of four 1980 Mack MC chassis outfitted by Anderson Engineering Co. with a 1,500-gpm pump, and a 400-gallon booster tank. Power is provided by a 500-hp Mack supercharged diesel engine. (Photo courtesy Bill Hattersley)

Tacoma bought this 1980 Mack CF, with a 50-foot Tele-Squrt tower, to run as Engine 9. (Photo courtesy Bill Hattersley)

The same Tacoma 1980 Mack CF—later the chassis was extended with another axle and stabilizing jacks added to carry a 75-foot Aerialscope. It then served as Truck 3. (Photo courtesy Bill Hattersley)

Newaukum, Washington, had Western States use this 1980 Mack three-axle chassis to build its 1,450-gallon tanker with a 1,250-gpm mid-ship pump. (Photo courtesy Bill Hattersley)

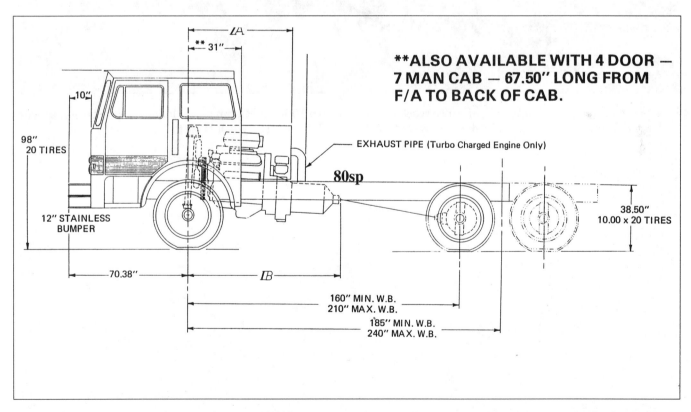

Segment of a drawing distributed by Spartan Motors, Inc., showing dimensions of its chassis and cab. A number of models were available to chassis outfitters. Spartan cabs were much larger than those on conventional commercial trucks, and became more necessary as safety regulations required firefighters to ride in cabs. (Photo courtesy Spartan Motors, Inc.)

Seattle purchased two 1980 Ward LaFrance trucks equipped with 100-foot Maxim aerial ladders. Note twin rear axles under rear-mount aerial. A Detroit diesel powered the truck. (Photo courtesy Bill Hattersley)

Chapter 4
1981-1990

*M*any apparatus had wide reflectorized stripes around their entire body to make them more visible at night. Reflectorized stripes were also placed on firefighters' clothing for the same purpose. Roll-up compartment doors came into use. Their main advantage was that individuals would not be tripping over them, which was a problem with swing-out doors, especially at night. New light and sound bars were mounted on top of cabs to improve and increase vehicles' warning signals.

Firefighters' unions began demanding "nondestructive testing" of aerial ladder devices in their respective departments. Most of the testing involved sophisticated—almost microscopic—examination of the ladder and its component materials.

In 1981, FDNY, as an experiment, painted 10 of its pumpers lime yellow. In 1982, a hazardous materials unit was built for FDNY, and the Superpumper System was removed from service. Apparently the nation's last salvage corps—and down to three stations—was the New York Fire Patrol, which bought a 1981 GMC.

In 1982, San Diego rebuilt a 1969 American-LaFrance quint by having it shortened and turned into a conventional pumper. The quint had proven to be unsatisfactory because of its weight and size. Drivetrains had to be replaced and the quints were involved in traffic accidents; in one incident the truck's bucket took out several windows on a parked school bus. The rebuild was done in American-LaFrance's Western states repair facility in Rialto, California, the only bidder on the job. The quint was one of four purchased in 1969-70 and San Diego then sent out for bids to convert the remaining three, which had been in reserve status since 1973.[1]

In 1985, the Metro-Dade County (Florida) Fire and Rescue Department placed a Bell 412 twin-engine helicopter into service. The helicopter carried both paramedic and fire suppression equipment. Intended uses included transporting seriously injured persons to hospitals, engaging in high-building rescue activity, and providing an observation post when dealing with major fires or hazardous materials incidents.[2]

In 1986, the Washington, D.C. fire department put into service two former army armored personnel carriers (on loan) outfitted with a monitor and a supply of pre-connected hose that would feed out the back and be supplied by another engine outside the field of (sniper) fire. The vehicles were for use in fires or other terrorist acts where firefighters needed protection from small-arms fire. The need for such a vehicle had been demonstrated in 1985 when a person was barricaded inside a burning building, firing a rifle.[3]

Bob Milnes, writing in early 1987, looked at the apparatus industry at that time. He believed that in the United States there were 250 fire apparatus builders, ranging from those who built three or four rigs per year, to the major manufacturers. A number of firms specialized in refur-

---

[1] *Firehouse* (January 1983), pp. 58-60.

[2] *Firehouse* (September 1985), p. 142.

[3] *Firehouse* (January 1987), pp. 68-69.

bishing. He thought that between 3,500-4,000 new apparatus would be delivered that year, with prices of some units exceeding $200,000. Lime yellow was accounting for only five percent of new deliveries. Orders for quints were expected to be high. St. Louis, in 1985, decided to equip all of its companies with quints, and Baltimore was combining engine and ladder companies into aerial tower quint companies. Large orders were also anticipated for hazardous materials and heavy rescue units. Nearly all units being delivered had seats inside cabs, with seatbelts, for all firefighters.[4]

In November 1987, Winston-Salem, North Carolina, did away with its "PSO" (public safety officer) program whereby individuals had served as both police and firefighters. The city then hired 51 new firefighters. At this time, fewer than 200 U.S. communities had these functions combined, and more than three-fourths of these communities were less than 25,000 in population.[5]

In 1989, a major earthquake hit San Francisco and in that city's Marina district both water and gas mains were broken. Fireboats were used to pump water inland, using five-inch hose carried on hose monitor trucks. Throughout the Bay area, fire crews were busy with rescue operations.

Many apparatus builders used chassis supplied by Duplex, Hendrickson, Oshkosh, Penfab, and Spartan. They all could accommodate the larger, enclosed, full-crew cabs that the fire service was demanding. There were many styles of cabs. Some Spartan literature of this era showed four styles of full-crew cabs, all of which tilted forward for access to the powertrain. One style had four doors, with two on each side, similar to an automobile. The second style was longer, with three seats, and seated 10 firefighters with the middle seat facing rearward. The third had four doors with the front ones on each side and two rear ones on the back side of the cab, where they would open on to the platform used by the operator of the "top-mount" pump controls. The fourth style could carry up to 10 firefighters and had a roof with two tiers. In front of the back seat there was room for individuals to stand, and a second windshield faced forward. A person standing in this area could look out windows on all sides, allowing the cab to be used as a command post.

American-LaFrance moved to a new plant in 1981, in a suburb of Elmira. The firm was a subsidiary of Figgie International, Inc., which had purchased it in 1966. American-LaFrance was encountering problems of dated designs, labor difficulties, high overhead, and was the target of a large class action lawsuit. In 1985, American-LaFrance notified its parent company that it was going to shut down for several months because of lack of orders. Figgie then closed the operation, keeping open its parts and service organization. It then moved portions of the fire apparatus building plant to Bluefield, Virginia, where Figgie had another subsidiary, Kersey Manufacturing Co. It then resumed production of fire apparatus with the name Kersey/American-LaFrance and introduced a new model, the "Century 2000." Sales were sluggish, and only 49 Century 2000s were built between 1985 and 1989. Most of American-LaFrance's big customers had moved to other makes of apparatus.

Beck delivered its first pumper in 1981. It was delivered to Cloverdale, California, where the firm was located. In 1983, the firm began building custom apparatus on Hahn chassis, and also outfitted a few rigs on Unimog chassis. (Unimogs are a rugged German-built off-road truck). In 1987, Beck became a subsidiary of the Ottawa Truck Co., known for its factory yard tractors.

Literature showing aerial ladders for Central States Fire Apparatus Inc., of Lyons, South Dakota, indicated that options available at the top of Central's aerial were 110 volt electricity and breathing air.

Crown's fire apparatus sales were sluggish and the firm was becoming better known for its line of school buses. In 1984, the firm moved from Los Angeles to nearby Chino.

Emergency One became a prominent supplier of apparatus nationwide during this decade. Its success was, to a certain extent, at the expense of some of the older manufacturers that would be dropping out of the market. Many of the nation's major cities were ordering batches of Emergency One apparatus, both custom and on commercial chassis. Large cities with Emergency One apparatus include: Boston, Chicago, Memphis, Philadelphia, Phoenix, Salt Lake City, Seattle, and Washington, D.C.

FMC turned out apparatus in both its Van Pelt and John Bean divisions (with the latter emphasizing high-pressure fog units). FMC's fire apparatus manufacturing operation moved in 1986 from Tipton, Indiana, to Orlando, Florida. In 1990, FMC shut down its fire apparatus division,

---

[4] *Firehouse* ((January 1987), pp. 30-31.

[5] *Firehouse* (August 1988), pp. 53-58.

although FMC remains in business, selling other products.

Hahn failed in 1990, after a rather quick decline. As late as 1986 it had 300 employees.

KME (Kovatch Mobile Equipment Corp.), a diversified manufacturer, began filling some large orders to big cities during this decade. It's headquartered in Nesquehoning, Pennsylvania.

LTI, which initially was an aerial ladder and platform supplier, was building complete apparatus. In 1986, it was acquired by Simon Engineering and became known as Simon-LTI. At the time, LTI was supplying about 20 percent of the aerial devices sold in the United States. In 1985, another firm with the name Simon, Simon Engineering Dudley Ltd., based in England (and possibly related) announced a 202-foot snorkel. It had three booms; the lowest boom had five telescoping sections. It was called a Super Snorkel and was mounted on a Terberg chassis, with a Volvo powertrain.[6]

In the mid-1980s, Mack stopped building custom apparatus and, in 1990, the truckmaker announced discontinuance of several chassis it built for other apparatus builders, citing low unit sales. Other Mack commercial chassis continue to be used by other outfitters.

Maxim struggled to stay in business during the 1980s and went through several owners. Maxim apparatus are no longer being built. In its day, Maxim had been a major supplier to several big city departments.

During this decade Pierce also became a major supplier of apparatus to cities both large and small. It marketed a series of custom apparatus—the Dash, Javelin and Lance. It also outfitted many units on commercial chassis.

This was a sad decade for Pirsch, which went bankrupt in 1986. At the time, the 129-year-old firm was the oldest privately owned corporation in Wisconsin. Considerable litigation and many claims from customers accompanied the bankruptcy. An attempt to revive the firm was unsuccessful.

Saulsbury, of Tully, New York, a well-known builder of custom rescue and mobile hospital bodies, began building firefighting apparatus on a number of chassis. Its market is nationwide.

Seagrave introduced several new models during the decade and made a number of deliveries of rear-mount aerials. These rear-mounts were on both custom and commercial chassis. Unlike many of the other "old-timers," Seagrave survived the decade.

Steeldraulic Products, of Rauzerville, Pennsylvania, began building ladder and rescue trucks. During this decade it made some deliveries on the West Coast.

In 1990, Sutphen celebrated its 100th anniversary. It had become best known for its trucks with aerial towers, which were popular with departments everywhere.

Westates received a large order from the California Office of Emergency Services for that agency's program of stationing apparatus in small communities. The communities may use the apparatus inside their own boundaries but must also supply it, with a crew, when needed elsewhere.

Western States continued in business, with most of its sales in Oregon.

This particular decade is notable because a number of "name" builders dropped out. Some went quickly, others sputtered to a halt. Firms that had been barely known a decade or two previously now dominated the market.

---

[6] *Firehouse* (January 1985), p. 24.

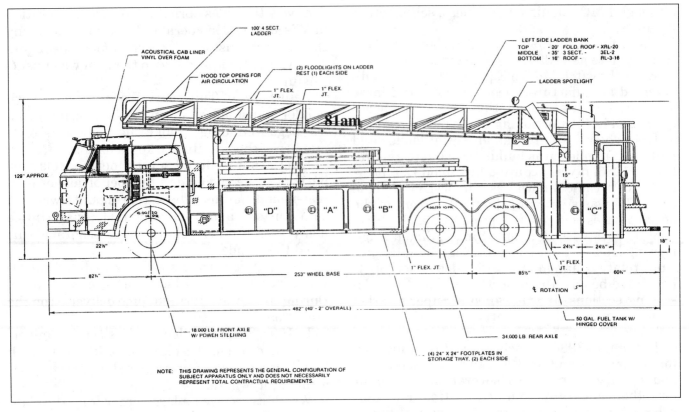

Circa-1980 drawing showing side view of American-LaFrance tandem aerial ladder. Ground ladders are removed from side. (Drawing courtesy American-LaFrance)

A 1981 American-LaFrance Century tandem rear-mount 100-foot aerial, in-service as Ladder 11 in Phoenix. (Photo courtesy Bill Hattersley)

FMC used a Spartan chassis to build this 1981 1,500-gpm pumper for Kenmore, Washington. It has a 500-gallon booster tank. (Photo courtesy Bill Hattersley)

A 1981 Ford/Emergency One 1,250-gpm triple combination pumper with a 500-gallon tank, used in Chicago. In 1992, the rig was rebuilt in the fire department's shops. Note soft suction hose on front bumper. (Photo courtesy Bill Friedrich)

Westates used a 1981 Freightliner chassis to build this 1,500-gpm pumper for Corte Madera, California. The booster tank carries 750 gallons. The driveway in front of the station where this rig is housed had to be replaced with thicker pavement because the new rigs in use were much heavier than those used when the station was built. (Photo courtesy Bill Hattersley)

Atlas used this 1981 GMC-Brigadier chassis to build Tanker 32 for Nashville. The tanker has a 300-gpm pump and 1,200-gallon water tank. A fold-up tank is on the side. (Photo courtesy Dick Adelman)

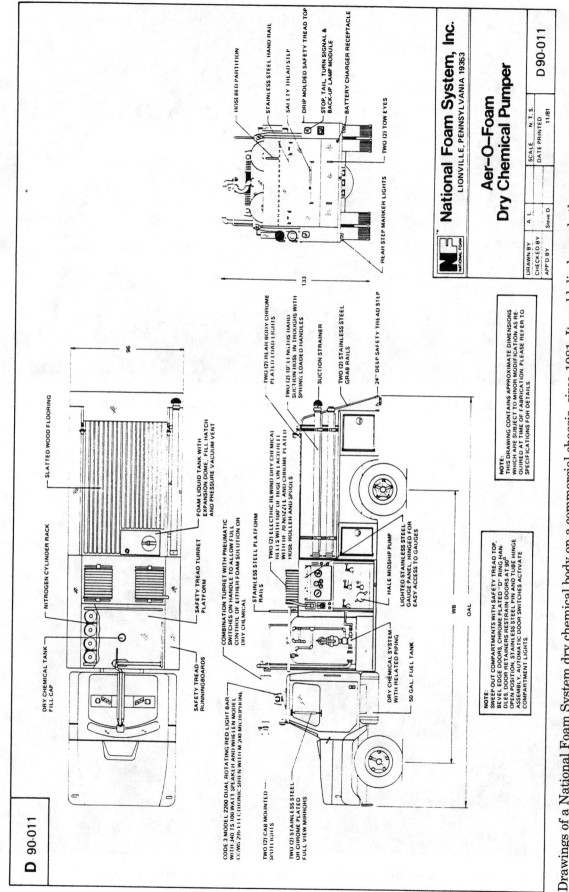

National Foam System, Inc.
LIONVILLE, PENNSYLVANIA 19353

**Aer-O-Foam
Dry Chemical Pumper**

D 90-011

DRAWN BY	A.L.	SCALE	N.T.S.
CHECKED BY		DATE PRINTED	11/81
APP'D BY	Steve D		

D 90-011

Drawings of a National Foam System dry chemical body on a commercial chassis, circa-1981. The foam would be pumped, and the dry chemicals would rely on compressed nitrogen to serve as an expellent. (Drawing courtesy National Foam System)

Dale City, Virginia, bought this 1981 Hahn that carried an 85-foot rear-mount tower ladder. Bottoms of outriggers are visible. (Photo courtesy Dick Adelman)

A 1981 Mack MC Series pumper with a sedan-type cab used by Maryland City, Maryland. Engine 271 has a 1,000-gpm pump, 500-gallon booster tank and front suction. (Photo courtesy Roland Boulet)

One of four Mack pumpers built on Mack MC chassis for Seattle. Anderson Engineering Co., of Vancouver, British Columbia, Canada, built the bodies. The trucks had 1,500-gpm pumps and 500-gallon tanks. They were diesel powered. (Photo courtesy Bill Hattersley)

San Francisco's Airport is protected by the low-profile 1981 Oshkosh outfitted by Grumman. It has a 1,500-gpm pump and a 500-gallon water tank. Its lower silhouette was necessary for use inside the airport's parking garages. (Photo courtesy Wayne Sorensen)

A commercial motor carrier was used to transport 1936 Pirsch Memphis Fire Department aerial trailers to Pirsch's Kenosha plant for rebuilding in 1981. Two aerials were rebuilt at this time, and were also joined with new tractors. (Photo courtesy Dick Adelman)

Marlboro, Maryland, operates this 1981 Seagrave rear-mounted aerial with a "W" cab. Note the control stand for the 100-foot aerial. (Photo courtesy Ray Stevens)

Folsum, California's 1981 Sutphen "quint" is powered by a Detroit diesel. It has a 100-foot aerial tower plus 164 feet of ground ladders. Its pump is rated at 1,250 gpm, and its booster tank carries 300 gallons. (Photo courtesy Wayne Sorensen)

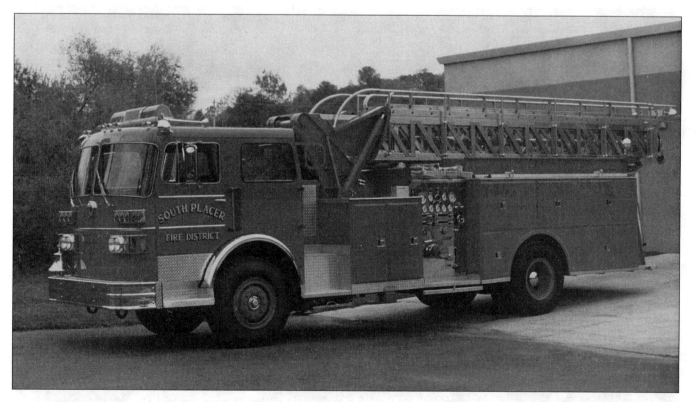

Sutphen built this 1981, 65-foot mini-tower for South Placer Fire District in Placer County, California. The mini-tower has a 1,250-gpm pump and 440-gallon booster tank. Power is from a 8V-92 Detroit diesel engine. (Photo courtesy Wayne Sorensen)

Western States used a Spartan chassis to build this 1981 pumper for Portland, Oregon. It has a 1,250-gpm pump, a 1,000-gallon water tank, and all-wheel drive. Pump controls are in front. Railing at far end of front bumper is to allow a rider to stand and direct a small stream of water while the truck is in motion. (Photo courtesy Bill Hattersley)

A 1982 American-LaFrance Century purchased by Lemont, Illinois. It carries a 1,500-gpm pump, 500 gallons of water, and a 75-foot rear-mount "Water Chief" aerial. (Photo courtesy Dick Adelman)

A 110-foot rear-mount aerial built for Chicago in 1982 by Emergency One, using a Hendrickson chassis. (Photo courtesy Bill Friedrich)

Nashville bought several 1982 FMC 1,500-gpm pumpers with 750-gallon tanks. They are mounted on Spartan chassis. (Photo courtesy Dick Adelman)

One of Nashville's 1982 FMC triple combination, 1,500-gpm pumpers. Built on Spartan chassis, these units carried 750 gallons of water. (Photo courtesy Dick Adelman)

Port Angeles, Washington, uses this 1982 Ford L-9000 outfitted by 3-D of Shawano, Wisconsin. It has a 1,500-gpm pump. (Photo courtesy Bill Hattersley)

A 1982 Grumman on a Duplex chassis used in Elizabethtown, Pennsylvania. It has a 95-foot rear-mount ladder. (Photo courtesy Roland Boulet)

Baltimore's Engine 43 is a 1982 Grumman 1,000-gpm pumper carried on a Duplex chassis. (Photo courtesy Roland Boulet)

Woodbridge, Virginia, ran this 1982 Hahn, which had a 106-foot aerial. The tractor also carried a 12,000-watt diesel generator behind the cab. (Photo courtesy Dick Adelman)

Washington, D.C., ran this 1982 Hahn as Engine 17. It has a 1,250-gallon pump and 500-gallon tank. (Photo courtesy Roland Boulet)

Washington, D.C.'s Engine 12 was a 1982 Hahn 1,250-gpm pumper with a 500-gallon water tank. Horizontal white stripe was to make unit more visible at night. (Photo courtesy Dick Adelman)

A 1982 King Seagrave built in Canada on a Penfab chassis. The pumper has a 1,000-gpm pump and 500-gallon booster tank, and runs as Engine 4 in Shelby County, Tennessee. (Photo courtesy Dick Adelman)

The cab of this 1982 Mack shows the influence of Renault, which had an ownership position in Mack. Saulsbury outfitted the rescue body and the rig was used in Orlando. Note small A-frame and winch in front. (Photo courtesy Dick Adelman)

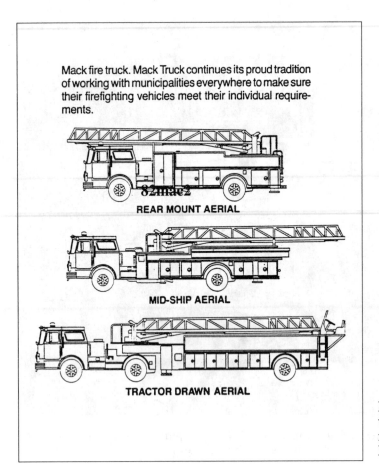

Mack fire truck. Mack Truck continues its proud tradition of working with municipalities everywhere to make sure their firefighting vehicles meet their individual requirements.

REAR MOUNT AERIAL

MID-SHIP AERIAL

TRACTOR DRAWN AERIAL

Drawing, from early-1980s Mack literature, shows the three styles of aerial ladder mounting: rear-mount, mid-ship, and tractor-drawn. (Drawing courtesy Mack)

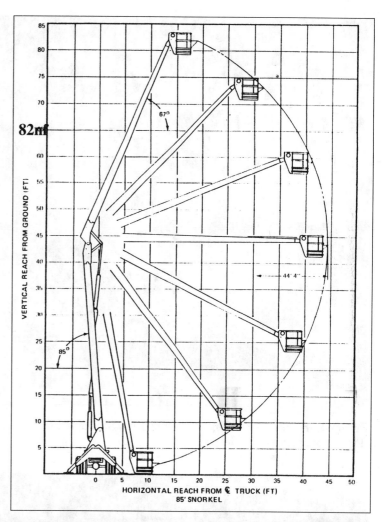

Rather than extending straight, snorkels have an "elbow." This drawing shows the pattern of their reach. (Drawing courtesy National Foam System)

Crash Truck 48 was based at Lambert Field, in St. Louis. It's built on a 1982 Spartan chassis, and has a 1,000-gpm pump. A foam gun is on top of the cab. (Photo courtesy Robert Pauly)

Engine 8 in Columbus, Ohio, was this 1982 Sutphen 1,000-gpm pumper. It also carried a 1,000-gallon booster tank. (Photo courtesy Dick Adelman)

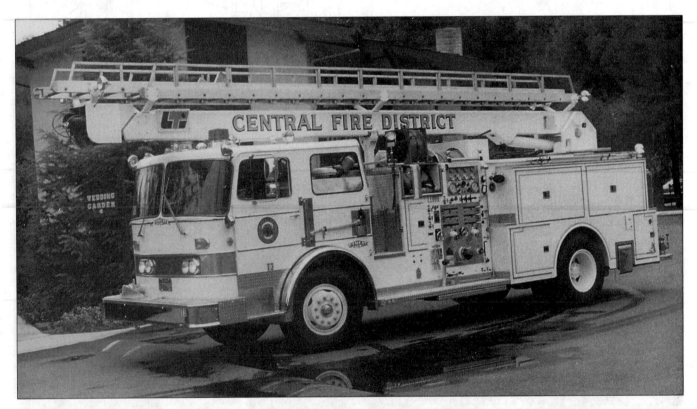

Truck 5 of the Central Fire Protection District in Santa Clara County, California, is this 1982 Van Pelt built on a Duplex chassis. It carries a 1,500-gpm pump, 400 gallons of water, and a 50-foot LTI rear-mount ladder. Power comes from a Detroit 8V-71 diesel. The rig is painted white. (Photo courtesy Wayne Sorensen)

Calistoga, California's 1983 Beck has a 1,000-gpm Darley pump and a 1,000-gallon water tank. It rides on a Hahn chassis. (Photo courtesy Wayne Sorensen)

Continental fire apparatus were built in Hopkinton, Massachusetts. This 1983 Continental triple combination was sold to Natick, Massachusetts. It carries a 1,250-gpm pump and a 500-gallon booster tank. (Photo courtesy Roland Boulet)

Chicago's Truck 42 is this 1983 Emergency One with a 110-foot rear-mount aerial carried on a Hendrickson chassis. (Photo courtesy Bill Friedrich)

Chicago's Truck 3 is a tall, 135-foot rear-mount aerial, built by Emergency One on a 1983 Penfab chassis. Banner on side of ladder promotes use of smoke detectors. (Photo courtesy Bill Friedrich)

Washington, D.C.'s Truck 1 was mounted on a 1983 Spartan six-wheel chassis. Truck 1 has a 135-foot rear-mount aerial and bodywork by Emergency One. (Photo courtesy Ray Stevens)

One of ten FMC-Van Pelts delivered to the Los Angeles City Fire Department in 1983. They were mounted on Spartan chassis and each carried a 1,500-gpm Hale pump, a pre-piped stainless deluge gun, and 500 gallons of water. (Photo courtesy FMC-Van Pelt)

Super Vacuum Manufacturing Co., of Loveland, Colorado, used an early-1980s International chassis for the rescue/ lighting body. Hydraulic power lifts the lights up to 16 feet. The lights rotate 360 degrees and tilt up to 110 degrees. The same hydraulic system can also be used to power other rescue tools that the truck carries. (Photo courtesy Super Vacuum Manufacturing Co.)

A 1983 Mack MC Series 1,500-gpm pumper delivered to Smyrna, Tennessee. Mack discontinued building complete fire apparatus in 1984. This pumper has a canopy tilt-cab and 1,000-gallon booster tank. (Photo courtesy Dick Adelman)

Working at a house fire is San Jose's Engine 26, a 1983 Mack CF triple combination 1,500-gpm pumper. Taking water from the hydrant supplies two service lines. (Photo courtesy Wayne Sorensen)

Pump panel on a 1983 Pierce-Arrow 1,500-gpm pumper in-service at Cole Collister Fire District near Boise, Idaho. Note word: "Starline," the Pierce dealer located in Boise. (Photo courtesy Milton G. Sorensen)

A 1983 Pierce-Arrow 50 Tele-Squrt with a 1,500-gpm pump and 500-gallon water tank in-service at the Whitney Fire District, south of Boise, Idaho. Note outriggers in place and open compartments showing air tanks. (Photo courtesy Milton G. Sorensen)

Columbus, Ohio's Ladder 12 is a 65-foot mini-tower quintuple with a 1500-gpm pump. Note the extended outrigger. Sutphen is the builder. (Photo courtesy Dick Adelman)

Belmont, Illinois, ran this 1984 American-LaFrance with a 1,500-gpm pump and a 1,000-gallon tank. Note mounted deck gun and red lenses on the inner twin headlights. (Photo courtesy Dick Adelman)

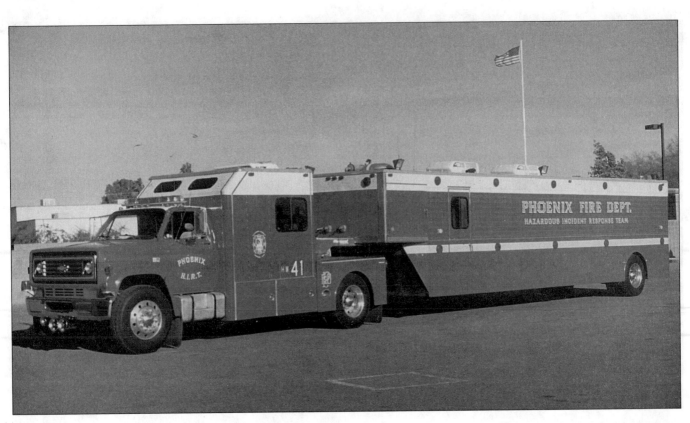

A 1984 Chevrolet tractor pulling a 1986 Chaparral trailer outfitted to serve as a hazardous materials incident response unit. It's used in Phoenix. (Photo courtesy Bill Hattersley)

Mercer Island, Washington's Ladder 1 is a 1984 Emergency One 110-foot rear-mount. (Photo courtesy Bill Hattersley)

Phoenix bought this 1984 FMC-Van Pelt. It has a 2,000-gpm pump, a 500-gallon tank, and a "stand-up" cab. (Photo courtesy Bill Hattersley)

A 1984 International chassis used by Grumman to build this 1,250-gpm triple combination for Paducah, to serve as Engine 1. The pump's capacity is 1,250 gpm and the booster tank holds 500 gallons. (Photo courtesy Dick Adelman)

A 1984 Mack chassis with a Ward fire apparatus body, used in Woodbury, Connecticut. The two large reels carry 5,000 feet of four-inch hose. The pump is rated at 1,500 gpm. (Photo courtesy Roland Boulet)

Circa-1984 Mack CF chassis used by Ward 79 to mount Bladenburg, Maryland's 1,500-gpm pumper. It also had a 500-gallon booster tank. This is similar to a model purchased in quantity by FDNY. (Photo courtesy Ray Stevens)

This 1984 Pirsch 1,000-gpm pumper with a 750-gallon booster tank is in-service as Memphis Engine 34. The pumper has front suction. Note the tire chains on rear wheels.

Santa Clara's Truck 1 was this quint built by Thibault, located in Pierreville, Quebec, Canada. It carries a 1,500-gpm Champion pump, and a 100-foot ladder.

Mid-1980s "view from the top" shows the Seagrave Apollo 105-foot aerial platform. (Photo courtesy Seagrave)

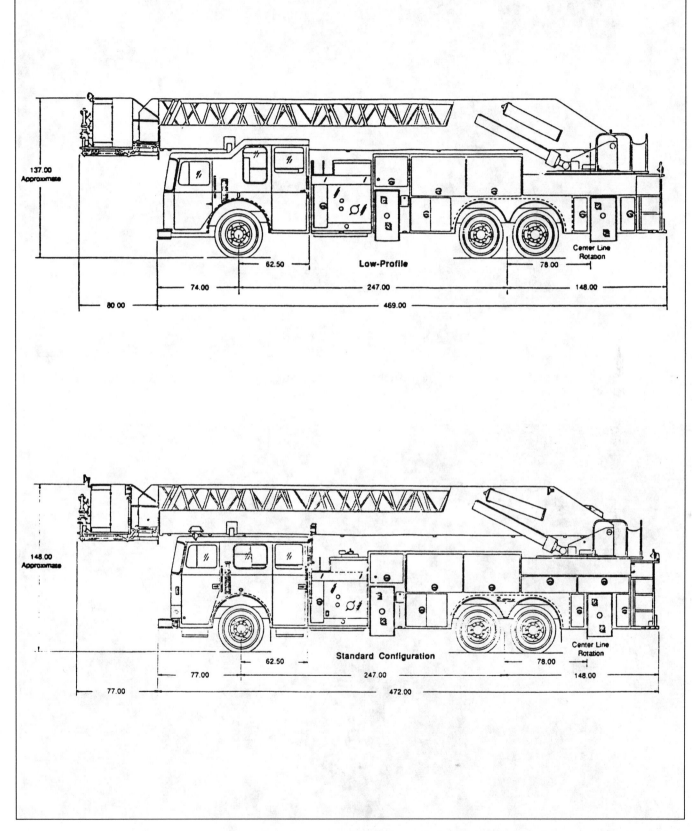

137.00 Approximate

62.50

Low-Profile

Center Line Rotation

74.00

247.00

78.00

148.00

80.00

469.00

148.00 Approximate

62.50

Standard Configuration

Center Line Rotation

77.00

247.00

78.00

148.00

77.00

472.00

Drawings of the mid-1980s Seagrave Apollo 105-foot aerial platforms, which were available in two overall heights. One reason for buying the shorter rig was to be able to fit inside existing fire stations. (Drawings courtesy Seagrave)

Chicago's Truck 27 is this 1985 Emergency One with a 95-foot rear-mount tower aerial carried on a Hurricane chassis. (Photo courtesy Bill Friedrich)

A 1985 FMC Roughneck Van Pelt with a 1,500-gpm pump and a 500-gallon water tank. It's carried on a Cummins-powered Crown chassis. It served as San Jose's Engine 12.

Wayne Township in Indiana has this 1985 FMC with a 102-foot rear-mount aerial, and a 1,500-gpm pump. It's carried on a Duplex chassis. (Photo courtesy Dick Adelman)

A 1985 Ford/Wheeled Coach ambulance was converted by the Chicago Fire Department into a high expansion foam unit. Work was done in 1994 by City International and the fire department's shops. The unit carries a Total Hi-EX foam generator that formerly was trailer-drawn. It's in service as Engine 28. (Photo courtesy Bill Friedrich)

Milwaukee's Engine 5 is this 1985 Ford/Pirsch. It has a 1,250-gpm pump, and a 400-gallon booster tank. Note the deck gun and the roll-up equipment compartment doors. (Photo courtesy Dick Adelman)

FMC used a 1985 Kenworth chassis to build Queenstown, Maryland's 1,000-gpm pumper with a 1,000-gallon tank. (Photo courtesy Ray Stevens)

Boise runs this 1985 Mack CF with a Baker 75-foot Aerialscope. Note the tandem rear axles and outrigger jacks. (Photo courtesy Bill Hattersley)

Avon-By-The-Sea, New Jersey, operated this 1985 Pirsch with a 100-foot rear-mount aerial. It has an enclosed Cincinnati cab. (Photo courtesy Dick Adelman)

This 1985 Pirsch tractor, tiller aerial is in service at Little Rock, Arkansas. The 110-foot aerial has a Cincinnati cab and enclosed tiller cab. (Photo courtesy Dick Adelman)

Saulsbury used a 1985 Spartan chassis to build this hazardous materials unit for Baltimore County, Maryland. (Photo courtesy Dick Adelman)

Partial view of Quakertown, Pennsylvania's Saulsbury rescue squad with compartment doors open. Note 12 air bottles, air hose reel, smoke ventilator, compressor and quartz lights. (Photo courtesy Saulsbury)

Tractor-drawn aerials are versatile for maneuvering in traffic. Phoenix's Ladder 1 uses the 1985 Seagrave tractor-drawn 100-foot aerial with box beam construction, which can lift heavy loads with the ladder fully extended. (Photo courtesy Bill Hattersley)

Western States used a 1985 Spartan chassis to build this 1,250-gpm pumper for Portland, Oregon. It has a 600-gallon booster tank and runs as Engine 5. (Photo courtesy Bill Hattersley)

Arlington County, Virginia, runs this 1985 1,250-gpm pumper built by Young. It has a 500-gallon tank. (Photo courtesy Dick Adelman)

Albany, New York's Engine 1 received the first series 2000 KALF American-LaFrance built on a Penfab chassis. The 1986 pumper has a 1,500-gpm American-LaFrance Twin Flow Pump and 750-gallon booster tank. (Photo courtesy Wayne Sorensen)

In 1986, Emergency One built this rear-mount 110-foot aerial for Salt Lake City, where it ran as Truck 14. (Photo courtesy Bill Hattersley)

Engine 3 in Washington, D.C. was this 1986 Emergency One 1,000-gpm pumper. It had a 500-gallon booster tank, front-mount suction, and top-mount pump controls. (Photo courtesy Ray Stevens)

Scott Valley, California, uses this 1986 FMC-Van Pelt mounted on a Hahn chassis. It has a 1,500-gpm pump and a 500-gallon water tank. (Photo courtesy Wayne Sorensen)

Carbon dioxide is used for fighting specialized fires. Pacific Gas and Electric, a northern California utility, donated $94,000 to the San Francisco Fire Department for the purchase of this CO_2 unit. The tank was built by Tamco and the rest of the work was by Reliable Fire Equipment. There is also a hydraulic crane that can reach to either side, and stabilizing jacks. Chassis is a 1986 Ford. (Photo courtesy Wayne Sorensen)

Seattle's 1986 Ford, which was reassigned and redesigned a number of times. The chassis carries a Waltco flatbed body on which was initially mounted an Ansul 3,000-pound nitrogen-expelled "Metl-X" system. It was originally purchased by Seattle City Light for use by the Seattle Fire Department in the event of a fire involving flammable metals associated with equipment used for decontaminating PCBs. The unit just described was assembled by the Transport Equipment Co. In 1987, the department shops converted the truck to a hazardous materials support unit, operating as half of a two-truck team. The Comet Corp. installed a body that could carry decontamination gear and barrels of waste. In 1992, the truck was again converted to a marine firefighting unit carrying equipment useful in combating fires aboard vessels moored alongside the pier. (Photo courtesy Dick Schneider)

San Francisco's Heavy Rescue 2 is a 1986 Ford chassis with bodywork by Welch. Power is from a Caterpillar diesel, 250-hp V-8 engine. (Photo courtesy Wayne Sorensen)

Olympia, Washington, runs this 1986 Grumman with a 1,500-gpm pump, 500-gallon tank, and a 50-foot Tele-Squrt. (Photo courtesy Bill Hattersley)

Engine 5 in Oakland, California, is this 1986 International, outfitted by Westates with a 1,500-gpm pump and a 500-gallon tank. (Photo courtesy Bill Hattersley)

The U.S. Army used this 1986 KME at the Presidio of San Francisco. It has a 1,250-gpm pump and carries 500 gallons of water. (Photo courtesy Wayne Sorensen)

One of five 1986 Kenworth/Steeldraulics pumpers delivered to San Francisco. It has a 1,500-gpm pump and a 500-gallon water tank. (Photo courtesy Thom Taggart)

A 1986 Kenworth chassis used by 4 Guys, Incorporated to build Leipsic, Delaware's 1,500-gpm pumper, which has a 1,000-gallon water tank and carries 1,800 feet of four-inch hose. (Photo courtesy Ray Stevens)

A 1986 Mack MC chassis used to build this 4,200-gallon tanker with a 1,500-gpm pump for Milton, Delaware. (Photo courtesy Ray Stevens)

San Jose's Engine 3 is a 1986 Pierce-Arrow 1,500-gpm pumper with a 500-gallon water tank. The powertrain is a 320-hp Cummins diesel engine with an Allison automatic transmission. (Photo courtesy Wayne Sorensen)

A 1986 Pierce-Arrow 1,500-gpm pumper tanker with a 3,000-gallon water tank built for Eagle, Idaho. The tanker has a top-mounted pump panel. The tanker is powered by 475-hp Detroit turbocharged diesel engine. (Photo courtesy Wayne Sorensen)

Syracuse's heavy rescue is a 1986 Saulsbury rescue body mounted on an International Paystar 5000 three-axle chassis. Note frame extension in front for power winch.

Baltimore purchased this 1986 Sutphen with a 100-foot aerial tower. It also has a 1,500-gpm pump. It serves as Aerial Tower 111. (Photo courtesy Dick Adelman)

Cambridge, Massachusetts, uses this 1986 Sutphen 100-foot, mid-mount tower ladder on three-axle chassis. (Photo courtesy Dick Adelman)

Portland, Oregon, bought this 1986 Western States quad built on a Spartan chassis. It has a 1,250-gpm pump with controls in the front, plus a 700-gallon tank. (Photo courtesy Bill Hattersley)

Beck built Monterey, California's 1987 1,500-gpm pumper with a 750-gallon water tank mounted on a Hahn chassis. (Photo courtesy Wayne Sorensen)

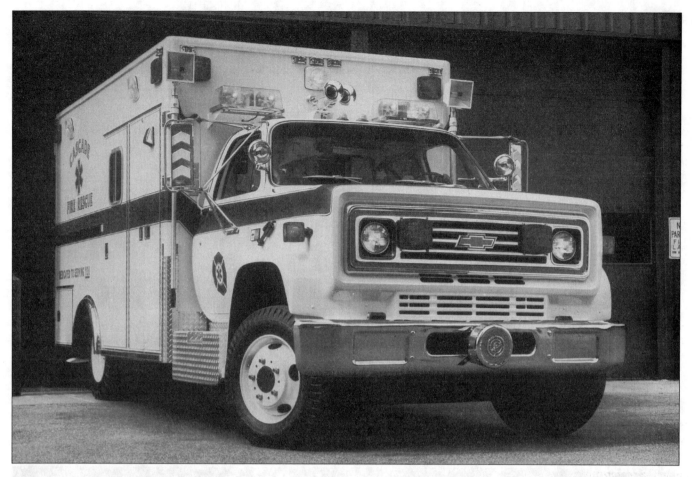

This medium-sized 1987 Chevrolet was featured in a factory photo. It has a "fire-rescue" body and a near-infinite number of lights. (Photo courtesy Chevrolet)

This 1987 Darley, built on a Spartan chassis, was sold to Yakima, Washington. It has a 1,500-gpm pump and 500-gallon tank. Top-mount pump control panel is on a platform behind cab, allowing operator to look in any direction. (Photo courtesy Bill Hattersley)

Phoenix uses this 1987 Emergency One pumper as Engine 5. It's on a Hush chassis and carries a 1,500-gpm pump and a 500-gallon water tank. (Photo courtesy Bill Hattersley)

Baltimore runs this 1987 FMC, carried on a Spartan chassis. Equipment includes a 1,000-gpm pump and a 750-gallon tank. Shown is Engine 32. (Photo courtesy Roland Boulet)

A 1987 Ford C high-pressure hose truck, with bodywork by Welch, equipped with a mounted turret pipe and Gorter high-pressure battery. It runs as High Pressure Battery 8 in San Francisco. (Photo courtesy Thom Taggart)

A 1987 Grumman on a Spartan chassis with a 1,500-gpm pump and a 200-gallon water tank, used in Twin Falls, Idaho. (Photo courtesy Bill Hattersley)

A 1987 Mack chassis mounted with a large water tank, built by General Steel Tank for Franklin, Tennessee. (Photo courtesy Dick Adelman)

Franklin, Tennessee, runs this 1987 Mack CF three-axle truck with an 85-foot Pitman Snorkel, 1,500-gpm pump and 500-gallon water tank. Bodywork was by FMC. (Photo courtesy Dick Adelman)

Large rebuilt pumper now used by a volunteer department. It's a 1987 Maxim custom 1,000-gpm pumper with a 750-gallon booster tank, used in Damascus, Maryland. (Photo courtesy Ray Stevens)

Nashville's Air Crash 3 is a 1987 Oshkosh T-3000. The T-3000 has two holding tanks. One tank holds 3,000 gallons of water and the second holds 410 gallons of AFFF light water concentrate which forms a vapor-suppressing seal and foam blanket, and is usually applied in conjunction with water from the booster tank. The unit has a remote hydraulic control turret. The handline provides both foam and water. (Photo courtesy Dick Adelman)

A 1987 Pierce-Lance 1,500-gpm pumper with split-cab design, 750-gallon water tank, and 100 gallons of foam in service at Naperville, Illinois. (Photo courtesy Dick Adelman)

A 1987 Seagrave Custom pumper with a 1,500-gpm Waterous pump built for Engine 7 of Portland, Oregon. It's equipped with a 1,000-gallon fiberglass booster tank and large sedan-type cab. (Photo courtesy Bill Hattersley)

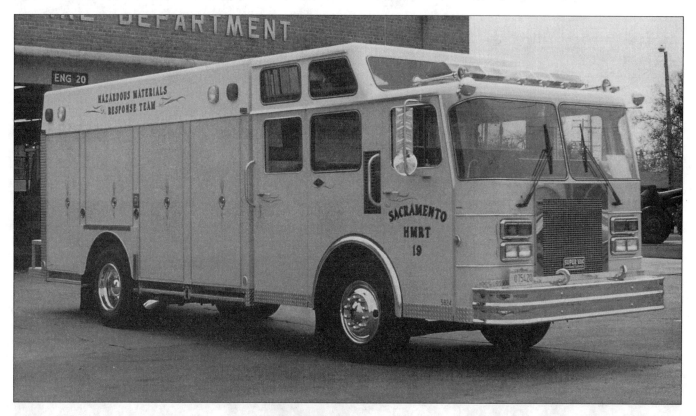

Sacramento's hazardous materials response team van built by Super Vac of Loveland, Colorado, on a 1987 Spartan chassis. The unit contains a generator, lights, hazmat library, and a cascade system air compressor and air purification system used to refill firefighters' air tanks. The truck is powered by a Detroit diesel engine. (Photo courtesy Wayne Sorensen)

Bower Beach, Maryland's 1988 American Eagle built on a Penfab three-axle chassis. It has a 1,000-gpm pump and a 3,000-gallon water tank. (Photo courtesy Ray Stevens)

A 1988 Ford C-8000 chassis used by Pirsch to build San Francisco's utility light unit. It has a 25-kw generator and six 250-foot reels of electrical cord with junction boxes. Although it looks like a Ford, the nameplate says "Pirsch." (Photo courtesy Wayne Sorensen)

Ogden, Utah's Engine 1 is a 1988 Duplex chassis with bodywork by Grumman. Engine 1 has a large crew cab, 1,500-gpm pump with a 750-gallon booster tank. (Photo courtesy Bill Hattersley)

Note the safety bars enclosing the rear seat on the 1988 KME pumper, operated by the Central Fire Protection District of Santa Clara County, California. The pumper has a 1,500-gpm pump and a 500-gallon booster tank.

Milwaukee's Truck 11 is this 1988 LTI 110-foot rear-mount aerial. It has a Duplex chassis and large cab. (Photo courtesy Dick Adelman)

Late-1980s Mack Model MC with bodywork by Saulsbury, a builder of custom rescue trucks. Livingston, New Jersey, operates this rescue rig, which carries a heavy-duty crane for emergency work. Note outrigger jack in rear. (Photo courtesy Saulsbury)

Jackson, Tennessee's Engine 2 was a 1988 Maxim 1,500-gpm triple combination with a 500-gallon booster tank and canopy cab. (Photo courtesy Dick Adelman)

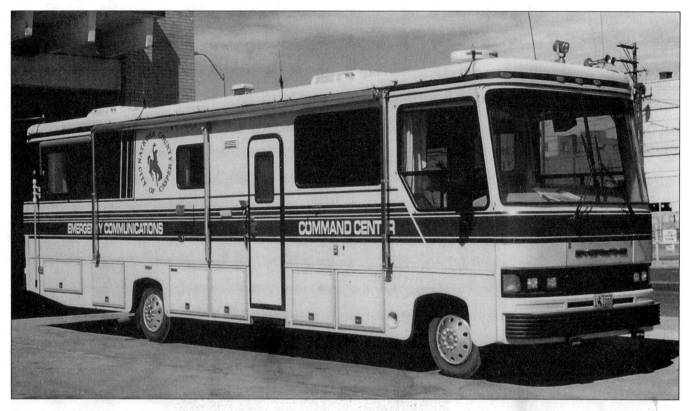

Casper, Wyoming, uses this command center, based on an Overland motorhome. (Photo courtesy Bill Hattersley)

A 1988 Pierce-Arrow 85-foot aerial platform with full aerial capabilities built for Truck 1 in San Jose. It's equipped with a 1,500-gpm pump and 250-gallon booster tank. The truck has hydraulically-operated outriggers located two forward and two rear of the tandem rear wheels. (Photo courtesy Wayne Sorensen)

Engine Company 38 of Cleveland uses this late-1980s 1,250-gpm Pierce-Arrow. It has telescoping quartz lights, and a large crew cab. (Photo courtesy John F. Sytsma)

A 1988 Pierce-Lance 75-foot aerial with 1,500-gpm pump and 300-gallon water tank in-service at Woodinville, Washington. (Photo courtesy Bill Hattersley)

Albany, New York's 1988 Medical Rescue Squad by Saulsbury is mounted on a Spartan chassis with large four-door cab. (Photo courtesy Ray Stevens)

Redmond, Washington, operates this 1988 Seagrave three-axle quintuple combination. It is equipped with a 1,500-gpm pump, 300-gallon water tank, a 110-foot rear-mounted aerial, and a four-door sedan cab. (Photo courtesy Bill Hattersley)

The Seattle Fire Department purchased four 1988 106-foot aerial trucks built by Simon-LTI, and three more identical trucks in 1992. Ladder 1 has a 1988 Spartan "Gladiator" tractor with a Simon-Ladder-Tower 106-foot, four-section hydraulically operated aerial. It's also equipped with a power takeoff-operated 10,000-watt generator mounted inside the trailer body supplying cable reels and operating power equipment. The powerplant is a 475-hp turbocharged Detroit diesel. The tiller seat is enclosed. (Photo courtesy Bill Hattersley)

Seattle's Ladder 12, a 106-foot rear-mount aerial delivered in 1988. It was built by Simon-LTI. The hydraulically operated, four-section, rear-mount aerial is mounted on a Spartan "Monarch" six-wheel chassis. It also has a power takeoff-operated 10,000-watt generator mounted inside the truck body. Ladder 12 has a four-door enclosed cab. (Photo courtesy Bill Hattersley)

Smeal Apparatus is made in Snyder, Nebraska. The firm used a Duplex chassis to build this 1,500-gpm pumper for Kenmore, Washington, in 1988. (Photo courtesy Bill Hattersley)

A 1988 Spartan tractor and 106-foot aerial trailer by LTI. In service as Truck 6 in San Francisco. (Photo courtesy Bill Hattersley)

Chicago rebuilt this 1970 Ward LaFrance in 1988 including the addition of a Ranger sedan cab and Emergency One bodywork. The unit has a 2,000-gpm pump, a 500-gallon booster tank, and carries 150 gallons of AFFF. (Photo courtesy Bill Friedrich)

San Francisco's 1974 American-LaFrance Pacemaker six-wheel snorkel tandem axle chassis was used by Westmark to build a fuel tank-truck in 1988. The truck carries 1,000 gallons of gasoline and 2,500 gallons of diesel fuel. It's stationed at San Francisco at Engine 9. (Photo courtesy Wayne Sorensen)

A 1988 White chassis outfitted by Marion Body Works, of Marion, Wisconsin, for Kirkland, Washington. It carries a 1,000-gpm pump and a 500-gallon water tank. (Photo courtesy Bill Hattersley)

Salt Lake City's Engine 1. It utilizes a 1989 Ottawa chassis with bodywork by American Eagle. It has a 750-gallon booster tank and a 1,750-gpm pump. (Photo courtesy Bill Hattersley)

This 1989 Autocar chassis was used by 4 Guys to build a 3,000-gallon tanker for Wicomico County, Maryland. It also has a 1,000-gpm front-mount pump. It's stationed in Mardela Springs. (Photo courtesy Dick Adelman)

Emergency One designed the Hush pumper with a rear engine to increase cab room and decrease cab noise. The Hush XL air horns and siren speakers are recessed in the vehicle's front bumper. The four-door cab holds up to 12 firefighters, seated and belted. This is Phoenix, Arizona's 1989 Emergency One pumper with a 1,500-gpm pump, 425-gallon booster tank and roll-up compartment doors. (Photo courtesy Bill Hattersley)

Nashville's Engine 29 is a 1989 Emergency One on a Cyclone chassis. This one carries a 1,500-gpm pump and a 500-gallon water tank. (Photo courtesy Dick Adelman)

Salt Lake City's Engine 14 is this 1989 Emergency One pumper on a Hurricane chassis. It is equipped with a Hale mid-ship Godiva 1,500-gpm pump, a 50-foot rear-mounted Teleboom, and elevated waterway pipe device. (Photo courtesy John F. Sytsma)

G. Paoletti, Inc., of San Leandro, California, built this hazardous materials and command unit for the Central Fire Protection District of Santa Clara County. The chassis was a 1989 Ford Cargo 800 with a diesel engine. It carries a generator and an oxygen tank filler. Equipment doors slide upward. (Photo courtesy Wayne Sorensen)

A 1989 Ford C extended cab chassis used by Pierce to build a 1,250-gpm pumper with 500-gallon water tank for Dublin, Georgia. Note top control pump panel. (Photo courtesy Dick Adelman)

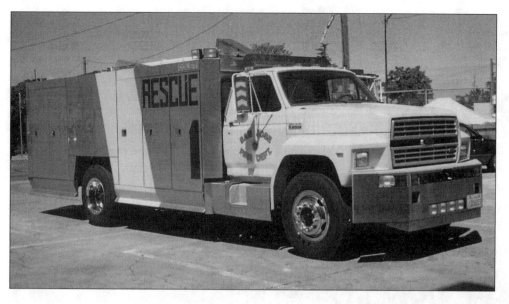

A 1989 Ford F-800 diesel, with bodywork by Colet of San Jose, which runs as Rescue Squad 1 in the San Jose Fire Department. (Photo courtesy Wayne Sorensen)

View of the top deck of a ladder platform. The two nozzles can deliver a total of 2,000 gpm. The truck is a 1989 KME quint that carries a 1,500-gpm pump and a 200-gallon tank. The truck is operated by the Central Fire Protection District of Santa Clara County, California. (Photo courtesy Wayne Sorensen)

A 1989 Hahn with a 1,500-gpm pump and 750-gallon booster tank, running in Abingdon, Maryland. (Photo courtesy Ray Stevens)

San Francisco's Ladder 1, a 1989 LTI with a 106-foot aerial ladder, throwing a masters stream from the top of the ladder. (Photo courtesy Thom Taggart)

San Francisco's Truck 10, a 106-foot LTI ladder pulled by a Duplex canopy cab tractor. (Photo courtesy Bill Hattersley)

The first 3-D pumper delivered to San Francisco was on a 1989 Mack CF chassis. The pumper is equipped with a 1,500-gpm pump and 500-gallon booster tank. (Photo courtesy Thom Taggart)

San Francisco's Truck 10, a 106-foot LTI ladder pulled by a Duplex canopy cab tractor. (Photo courtesy Bill Hattersley)

The first 3-D pumper delivered to San Francisco was on a 1989 Mack CF chassis. The pumper is equipped with a 1,500-gpm pump and 500-gallon booster tank. (Photo courtesy Thom Taggart)

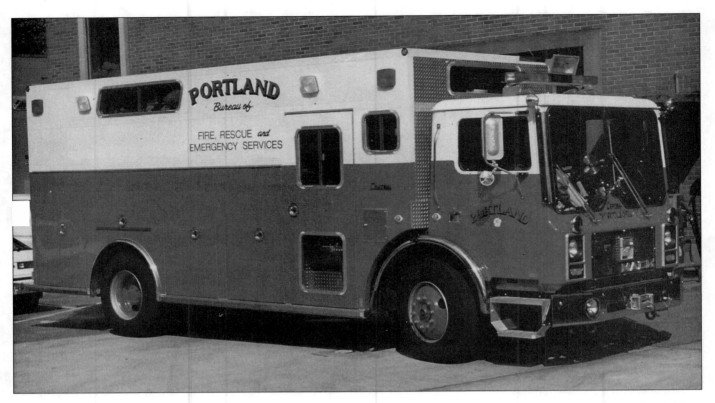

Portland, Oregon, used this 1989 Mack ACC with a Central States Body as a rescue truck. (Photo courtesy Bill Hattersley)

Kent, Washington, uses this 1989 Pierce-Lance 1,500-gpm pumper equipped with a 500-gallon water tank and Emergency Medical Service cab, meaning that it could also be employed as an ambulance. (Photo courtesy Bill Hattersley)

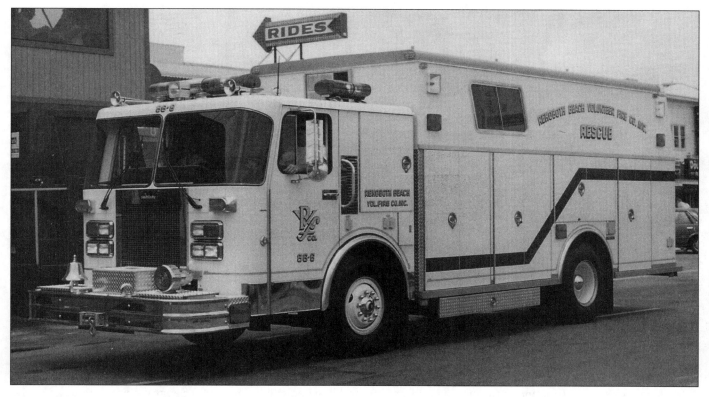

Rehoboth Beach, Delaware, operates this Saulsbury Rescue Squad mounted on a Spartan chassis. (Photo courtesy Ray Stevens)

A 1989 Seagrave with a rear-mount 110-foot aerial, used in Prince Georges County, Maryland. (Photo courtesy Dick Adelman)

A ladder truck's main function is to serve as a lifesaving and rescue device. This 1989 Seagrave rear-mounted aerial serves Puyallup, Washington. The truck has a five-man canopy cab and a piped waterway. (Photo courtesy Bill Hattersley)

Boise, Idaho, operates this "J" cab or flat front 1989 Seagrave as Engine 5. It is equipped with a 1,500-gpm pump, 500-gallon booster tank and four-door sedan cab. Note that the ground ladders are on an automatic rack. (Photo courtesy Wayne Sorensen)

A 1989 Seagrave pumper with a "J" cab. The doors on the "J" cab are full length versus the shorter doors on the "H" and "W" series cabs. Kentland, Maryland's pumper is equipped with a 1,250-gpm pump and 500-gallon booster tank. (Photo courtesy Ray Stevens)

Hi-Tech of Oakdale, California, built this foam truck for San Jose, using a 1990 Ford chassis. It has a 750-gpm pump.

Santa Clara, California's Engine 7 is a 1990 KME with a 1,500-gpm pump and a 500-gallon water tank. (Photo courtesy Wayne Sorensen)

San Francisco Engine 25 is a 1990 3-D with a four-door cab, a 1,500-gpm pump, and a 500-gallon tank. (Photo courtesy Bill Hattersley)

Two-piece rescue company of Jacksonville, mounted on circa-1990 Ford L-8000 diesel and a Ford L-9000 by Saulsbury. Note the quartz lights and the large side door on the heavy rescue truck. Both trucks have roll-up doors. (Photo courtesy Saulsbury)

A 1990 Ford/Emergency One 1,250-gpm pumper built for use in Washington, D.C., where it ran as Engine 27. A modular rear crew compartment was placed behind the three-man tilt-cab. It has a 500-gallon booster tank, and front-mount suction. (Photo courtesy Dick Adelman)

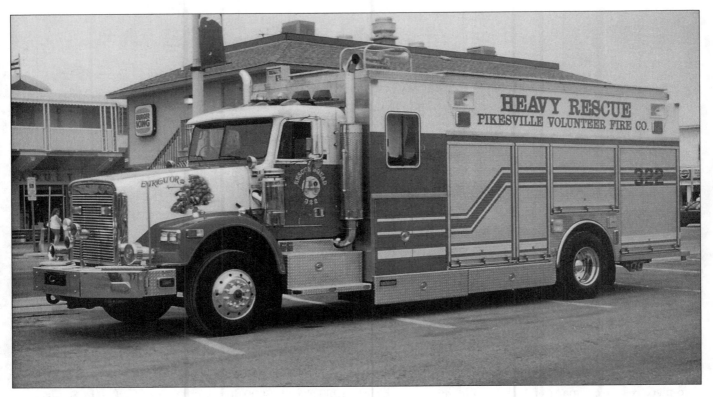

Pikesville, Maryland, operates this circa-1990 Freightliner/Saulsbury Heavy Rescue Squad. Note the roll-up compartments. (Photo courtesy Ray Stevens)

Longwood, Pennsylvania, ran this 1990 Grumman that carried a 1,500-gpm pump, 500 gallons of water, and a 65-foot Tele-Squrt on a Spartan chassis. (Photo courtesy Ray Stevens)

Point Pleasant, New Jersey, operates this 1990 Hahn with a 1,500-gpm pump, 500-gallon tank, and 20 gallons of foam. (Photo courtesy Ray Stevens)

A Navistar International 4000 series with a Travelcrew four-door cab used by Saulsbury to build Columbia, Missouri's Rescue Squad. (Photo courtesy Saulsbury)

Santa Clara County, California's Engine 3 is built on a 1990 short wheelbase KME chassis and carries a 1,500-gpm pump and a 750-gallon booster tank. Short wheelbase units are often used in areas with curved mountain roads.

A 1990 KME 1,500-gpm triple combination short wheelbase pumper in service as Engine 3 of Los Gatos, California. Engine 3 is equipped with a 725-gallon water tank and four-door cab, with two side doors and two rear doors. Note the roll-up compartment doors. (Photo courtesy Wayne Sorensen)

Livermore, California, uses this 1990 KME Renegade 1,500-gpm pumper with a 500-gallon booster tank. The raised-roof cab seats eight firefighters and is both padded and air-conditioned. (Photo courtesy Wayne Sorensen)

Close-up shows deck gun in operation. (Photo courtesy Wayne Sorensen)

Truck 2 in San Francisco is a 1990 Spartan tractor pulling a 106 LTI aerial. The ground ladders are wooden. On rear tiller is a bubble to improve the tillerman's side visibility. (Photo courtesy Thom Taggart)

San Francisco's Truck 5, a 1990 Spartan tractor pulling a 106-foot LTI aerial trailer. Ground ladders are made of wood, because of the many overhead trolley wires in San Francisco. (Photo courtesy Thom Taggart

Arlington County, Virginia, purchased this 1990 LTI aerial ladder trailer and used a 1979 Hahn four-door tractor to pull it. Note roll-up equipment doors. (Photo courtesy Dick Adelman)

Boise, Idaho, runs this 1990 LTI with a 110-foot aerial ladder and an enclosed tiller cab. (Photo courtesy Bill Hattersley)

Brown Deer, Wisconsin, a suburb of Milwaukee, runs this LTI quint carried on a Duplex chassis. It has a 110-foot, rear-mount aerial, a 1,500-gpm pump, and a 200-gallon booster tank. (Photo courtesy Dick Adelman)

Marion Body Works built Engine 22 for Portland, Oregon, on a Spartan chassis. It has a 1,500-gpm pump and a 500-gallon booster tank. (Photo courtesy Bill Hattersley)

Nashville's Engine 32 is a 1990 Mack pumper with bodywork by Quality. The booster tank carries 1,000 gallons of water and the pump is rated at 1,500 gpm. (Photo courtesy Dick Adelman)

Baltimore County ran this 1990 Mack chassis outfitted by Ward 79, successor to Ward LaFrance. The pump on this unit was rated at 1,250 gpm and the booster tank carried 500 gallons. (Photo courtesy Ray Stevens)

Nashville, Tennessee, purchased this 1990 Ottawa tractor with a four-door cab to pull its 1973 American-LaFrance 100-foot aerial trailer. (Photo courtesy Dick Adelman)

Auburn, California, placed in-service this water tender mounted on a 1990 Peterbilt three-axle chassis, equipped with a 1,000-gpm pump and 3,000-gallon water tank outfitted by XME. (Photo courtesy Bill Hattersley)

Memphis operates this 1990 Pierce pumper as Engine 5. It has a 1,500-gpm pump, a 500-gallon booster tank, and a mounted turret pipe. A tray behind the front bumper holds suction hose connected to front-mount suction opening. (Photo courtesy Dick Adelman)

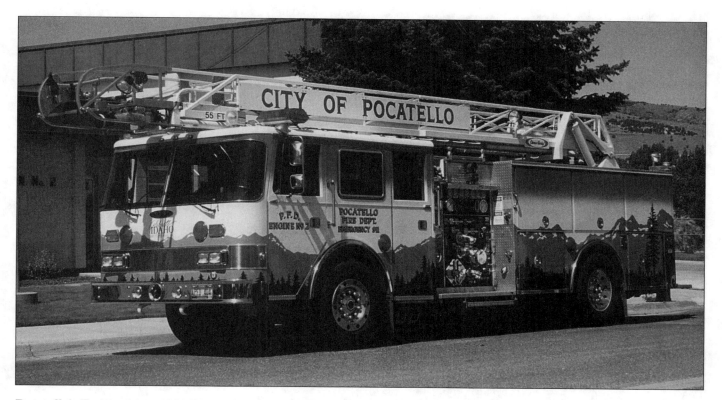

Pocatello's Engine 2 is a 1990 Pierce-Arrow quint. The pump is rated at 1,500 gpm, the booster tank holds 500 gallons, and the 55-foot ladder is by LTI. Power is provided by a Detroit diesel 8V-92A engine. The truck was painted red, white, and blue-gray to help celebrate the state's centennial. (Photo courtesy Wayne Sorensen)

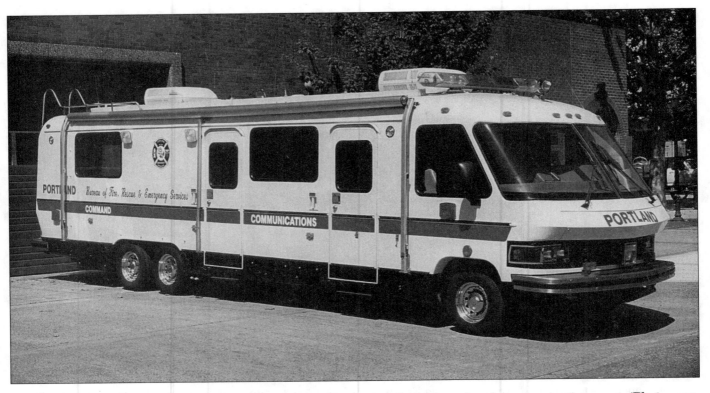

Portland, Oregon, uses this 1990 Revcom as a fire and rescue mobile command and communications post. (Photo courtesy Bill Hattersley)

A Simon-Duplex/FMC pumper with a 1,500-gpm pump and a 500-gallon water tank. The truck is operated by the Saratoga, California, Fire Department. (Photo courtesy Wayne Sorensen)

The Union Fire Co. in Bensalem Township, Bucks County, Pennsylvania, owns this 1990 LTI quint with a 1,500-gpm pump, a 400-gallon water tank, and a 75-foot LTI rear-mount aerial. It's carried on a Spartan chassis. (Photo courtesy Ray Stevens)

A 1990 Sutphen with a 100-foot tower ladder used in Chestertown, Maryland. It carries a 1,250-gpm pump and a 300-gallon booster tank. (Photo courtesy Ray Stevens)

San Francisco's Engine 6 is this 3-D 1,500-gpm pumper built on a Spartan Gladiator chassis. It has a 500-gallon booster tank, and is shown at a drill with the Bay Bridge in the background. (Photo courtesy Thom Taggart

The firm of 3-D, in Shawano, Wisconsin, delivered eight pumpers to the San Francisco Fire Department in 1990. They were built on Spartan chassis and have four-door crew cabs. This is Engine 31. (Photo courtesy Wayne Sorensen)

One of four Westates pumpers on 1990 Mack chassis delivered to San Jose. It carries a 1,500-gpm pump and a 500-gallon water tank. (Photo courtesy Wayne Sorensen)

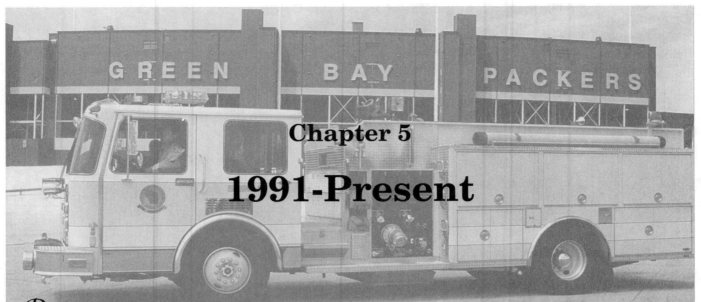

Chapter 5

1991-Present

*D*uring the first half of this decade, many apparatus deliveries were made by firms that were barely acknowledged in the early chapters of this book. Most apparatus had fully enclosed cabs that carried the entire crew. Seating requirements took into account that many firefighters who suited up were also carrying backpack air supplies. Cabs were often air-conditioned, which helped those riding and also those taking breaks while at the fire scene. Some apparatus had small rearward facing video cameras mounted on the back giving the driver a view to the rear.

The lime green color was losing ground with more deliveries made of the traditional red apparatus. However, recent deliveries usually have a white or reflectorized stripe parallel to the bottom. "911" has become the near-universal telephone number to dial for emergencies and dispatchers handle fire, police, and EMS calls, and rely heavily on computers to make assignments.

Phoenix installed an Automatic Vehicle Location (AVL) system whereby each piece of apparatus can be "tracked" by satellites. The device carried on the trucks emits a signal that can be identified by several satellites, which determine the apparatus' latitude and longitude by triangulation. It is also possible to determine the truck's speed. Positioning is within 300 yards of the truck's exact location 99.9 percent of the time.[1] The system's main value is dispatching to a second fire while apparatus are already en route to the first fire.

Firefighters carried individual radios so they could be in constant contact with their superiors and other firefighters. This was useful at the site of fires as well as while performing building inspections.

In many localities, an increased portion of time is spent responding to medical emergencies and to hazardous material spills. One engine was shown with a household bathroom shower head mounted high and on one side, to be used to wash down personnel after handling hazardous materials.[2] Departments operate EMS vehicles that are more sophisticated than traditional ambulances because a variety of treatments can be provided while the patient is en route to the hospital.

Large departments are also purchasing specialized vans to deal with hazardous materials incidents, although no one standardized or common design has emerged. There are two apparent steps to responding to an incident. The first is to determine the hazardous material involved and the extent of the danger. The second step is to decontaminate the site, which means neutralizing the hazards and removing other materials that might contribute to worsening the hazard. Laptop computers can access large databases with information about all chemicals and chemical products. Other stored data that might be accessed would be lists of other community resources that might be called upon to give aid.

A wildfire in the hills above Oakland, California, destroyed more than 2,000 dwellings. There were delays in calling for initial backup support and the

---

[1] Firehouse (August, 1994), p. 37.

[2] Firehouse (January, 1995), p. 70.

fire was soon out of hand. In some areas water supplies failed because the fire had destroyed electric lines that provided power for pumps. Fire apparatus had problems traveling in the area because of parked cars restricting the width of narrow roads, and the auto traffic caused by people fleeing their homes. An earthquake in Southern California and a number of hurricanes in coastal regions of the south required large-scale rescue efforts.

In 1995, the Port of Montreal, Quebec, Canada, lost the service of a privately owned tugboat that had also been outfitted for firefighting. In its place, the port put into operation a fire barge onto which two pumpers, an aerial platform, and an aerial ladder truck would be driven after having been dispatched from a nearby station. A separate tugboat would then tow the loaded barge to the fire site. The pumpers would draft from the river and the aerial trucks could be used for either attacking the flames on a ship, or for rescue. Each piece of apparatus is assigned a specific spot on the barge. The pumpers, for example, must be located so that their suction hoses do not come close to the tugboat's propellers.

Figgie International, which owned American-LaFrance, ceased production of fire apparatus in 1994. At the start of this book, American-LaFrance was the nation's best-known apparatus builder. Its cab-forward models, actually introduced in the late-1930s, were eventually copied by all its competitors. In 1995, Freightliner acquired some limited rights to American-LaFrance and, in 1996, announced the "American LaFrance Eagle" fire apparatus chassis and cab, built on Freightliner's well-known heavy truck chassis. The intent is to have the chassis used by apparatus outfitters. Initially, four different cab styles are available. An option is a factory-installed mid-ship Hale pump. At this writing, American LaFrance Eagle is the only fire chassis available with an installed pump.

Beck went out of business in 1992, after having built 402 pieces of apparatus. Crown Coach closed operations in early 1991 after three years of losses. The Boardman Co., of Oklahoma City, a longtime regional supplier of apparatus, went out of the fire truck business in 1995 and continues as a sheet metal works.

In 1992, FMC closed the former Van Pelt operation in Oakdale, California. Several one-time Van Pelt employees formed a new firm, called Hi-Tech Apparatus, which initially refurbished fire apparatus. Refurbishing includes building new or altered bodies, repairing pumps and booster tanks, and providing preventative maintenance service. Soon Hi-Tech began building both custom fire engines as well as outfitting apparatus on commercial chassis.

In 1996, Oshkosh Truck Corp. bought Pierce, located in nearby Appleton. The move for Oshkosh was an attempt to become less dependent upon military orders.

In 1994, Waterous, a well-known builder of pumps, celebrated its 150-year anniversary. Early in the century the firm had built apparatus also, but then decided to concentrate on pumps.

At the middle of the decade, here's a list of most of the firms outfitting fire apparatus. If we've missed any, let us know via our publisher so we might include them in any future books. The list includes: Becker, Casper, Wyoming; Boise Mobile Equipment Co., Boise, Idaho; Darley, Melrose Park, Illinois; Emergency One, Ocala, Florida; Farrar Co., Woodville, Massachusetts; Hi-Tech, Oakdale, California; HME, Wyoming, Michigan; KME, Nesquehoning, Pennsylvania; Luverne Fire Apparatus, Luverne, Minnesota; Marion Body Works, Marion, Wisconsin; Pierce, Appleton, Wisconsin; S & S Apparatus Co., Fairmont, Indiana; Saulsbury, Tully, New York; Seagrave, Clintonville, Wisconsin; Simon-LTI, Ephrata, Pennsylvania; Smeal Fire Apparatus, Snyder, Nebraska; Super Vac, Loveland, Colorado; Sutphen, Springfield, Ohio; 3-D, Shawano, Wisconsin; Towers Fire Apparatus, Freeburg, Illinois; Utah LaGrange, Inc., Orem, Utah; Westates, Hayward, California; Western States, Cornelius, Oregon; Westmark, Ceres, California; and Young Fire Equipment Corp., Buffalo, New York.

This ends the second of two volumes. Which firms mentioned in the first volume—which ended in 1950—exist today? Seagrave has been a major supplier of fire apparatus for the entire century, and initially built hand- and horse-drawn ladder trucks. A sentence in its current literature states: "Seagrave, the greatest name in fire apparatus, since 1881." Waterous survives as a maker of quality pumps. Luverne, Young, and Darley were also mentioned in Volume One although none was considered to be a major player. A few other firms mentioned in this volume existed prior to 1950 although they delivered few or no apparatus at that time. A few body builders who often helped apparatus outfitters also survived including Jacob Press of Chicago and Geo. Heiser of Seattle. Mack continues to be a prominent builder of trucks, but no longer turns out its own line of fire apparatus. In both the truck chassis industry and the truck body industry there appears to be more stability over the century than has been the case with fire apparatus builders and outfitters. The reasons as to why this is so would be an interesting topic to study.

Montreal has its fire apparatus driven on a barge, and the barge is then towed to the fire site. (Port of Montreal)

Dixon, California, has in service this Beck-built quintuple combination on a 1991 Ottawa chassis equipped with a 1,500-gpm pump, 500-gallon water tank and a 55-foot Fire Stix ladder. (Photo courtesy Bill Hattersley)

A 1991 Chevrolet Utilmaster Van, used as a Hazardous Materials unit by the San Francisco Fire Department. (Photo courtesy Wayne Sorensen)

California's Silicon Valley is a center of semiconductor manufacturing, an industry that relies on many hazardous materials. San Jose put this Hazardous Incident Team unit into operation in 1991. It was built by Colet Special Vehicles at a reported cost of $350,000. It was removed from service in 1993 because of brake and electrical problems.

A 1991 Emergency One 95-foot platform built for Oxon Hill, Maryland. Power is provided by a Detroit diesel. The underslung jacks spread 13 feet, 8 inches. (Photo courtesy Ray Stevens)

In 1991, Emergency One supplied Seattle with nine 1,500-gpm Hale pump triple combination pumpers, built on Spartan "Gladiator" chassis. They had top-mounted controls. Shown is Engine 5 equipped with a 500-gallon booster tank with an internally plumbed monitor that can be used on the apparatus deck or removed and set on a stand for portable operation. The truck is powered by a 400-hp turbocharged Detroit diesel. (Photo courtesy Bill Hattersley)

Emergency One built this interesting quintuple combination on its Hush chassis for Milton, Washington. It's equipped with a 1,500-gpm pump, 500-gallon water tank and 50-foot Strata spear ladder. (Photo courtesy Bill Hattersley)

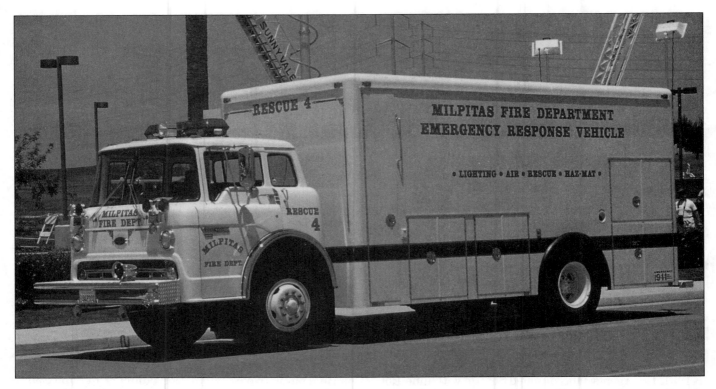

Milpitas, California's Rescue 4 is mounted on a 1991 Ford chassis, outfitted by G. Paoletti. This emergency response vehicle includes lighting, air, rescue and equipment and materials for hazardous material incidents. (Photo courtesy Wayne Sorensen)

A 1991 Ford chassis with Paoletti bodywork, 400-gpm pump, and 500-gallon water tank in-service in Alameda, California, as Engine 52. (Photo courtesy Bill Hattersley)

Milton, Delaware, operates this 1991 Grumman built on a Spartan chassis. The booster tank carries 1,000 gallons and the pump is rated at 1,500 gpm. (Photo courtesy Ray Stevens)

Pierce used a 1991 Navistar International 4000 Series with four-door Travelcrew cab for Sharon, Tennessee's Engine 2. It has a 1,250-gpm pump and 750-gallon water tank. (Photo courtesy Dick Adelman)

Two views of a 1991 International Navistar 4x4 chassis used by Westmark to build this 350-gpm patrol with a 500-gallon water tank. It functions as Patrol 1 of Central Fire Protection District of Santa Clara County, California. (Photo courtesy Wayne Sorensen)

Pump is mounted in rear. (Photo courtesy Wayne Sorensen)

The Aetna Hose and Hook and Ladder Company of Newark, Delaware, runs this 1991 KME Falcon Terminator with a 1,500-gpm pump and a 750-gallon booster tank. (Photo courtesy Ray Stevens)

Modesto, California, bought this 1991 LTI pulled by an Olympian four-door tractor. (Photo courtesy Bill Hattersley)

Airplane crashes often occur short distances from the airport in areas not always accessible by road. This early-1990s Oshkosh, with two front and two rear axles is used by Wittman Field, in Winnebago County, Wisconsin. Pump is at the front of trailer and the hose on roof carries foam to nozzles above cab. (Photo courtesy Oshkosh Truck Corp.)

A 1991 Peterbilt Model 320 tilt-cab with a Belton Body in-service as Seattle's Hazardous Materials Unit 77. Equipment cabinets carry protective gear, detection and decontamination equipment, and disposal supplies. Truck carries a "CAMEO" computer system for determining properties of spilled materials and calculating degree or extent of contamination risk. A 7,500-watt generator supplies power to four telescoping quartzide lamps mounted in the corners of the van body. (Photo courtesy Bill Hattersley)

A 1991 Pierce-Lance 100-foot LTI rear-mount aerial ladder on a three-axle chassis in-service at Elko, Nevada. It's equipped with a 1,750-gpm pump and 500-gallon water tank. (Photo courtesy Wayne Sorensen)

Portland, Oregon, runs this 1991 Sutphen 100-foot tower aerial as Truck 1. It has twin monitors for delivering two streams. It has a leveling system. (Photo courtesy Bill Hattersley)

Bay District, in Maryland, remounted a 1974 Grove 100-foot aerial on a 1992 three-axle American-LaFrance Penfab chassis. (Photo courtesy Dick Adelman)

A 1992 Carlin Mobile Communications Center built for the California Department of Forestry. The emergency support unit was built in Fresno. (Photo courtesy Wayne Sorensen)

Darley used this 1992 Spartan chassis to build a 1,500-gpm pumper with 500-gallon water tank for Yakima. (Photo courtesy Bill Hattersley)

Alderwood, Washington's Engine 1 is a 1992 Darley 1,500-gpm pumper with 500-gallon water tank on a Spartan chassis, and with a four-door cab. (Photo courtesy Bill Hattersley)

Engine 6 at Naperville, Illinois, is this 1992 Emergency One 1,500-gpm pump, mounted on a Hush chassis. It carries 1,000 gallons of water and 100 gallons of foam. (Photo courtesy Dick Adelman)

Winters, California's Engine 1 runs a 1,000-gpm pumper with a 500-gallon water tank mounted on a 1992 Ford Cargo chassis by Westates. (Photo courtesy Bill Hattersley)

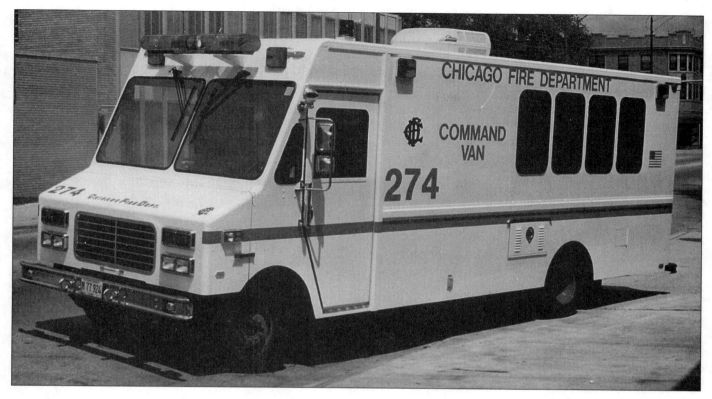

Command van used by Chicago's Fire Department. A Utilmaster van body was placed on a 1992 Ford chassis. The rig carries on Onan six-kw diesel generator. (Photo courtesy Bill Friedrich)

Milwaukee's Engine 12 is a 1992 Darley 1,500-gpm pumper with a 500-gallon water tank mounted on a Ford L four-door chassis with roll-up compartment doors. (Photo courtesy Dick Adelman)

Portland, Oregon, operates this state-owned 1992 Ford, with a body by Hesse, as Oregon's Region 6 Hazmat Team. (Photo courtesy Bill Hattersley)

An early 1990s GMC with a Pierce pumper body serving as Engine 65 in Houston. (Photo courtesy Pierce)

Two views of a 1992 Hi-Tech 1,500-gpm pumper on a Spartan chassis. It serves as Los Gatos Engine 6 in the Santa Clara County Central Fire Protection District. It carries 750 gallons of water and two foam units. (Photo courtesy Wayne Sorensen)

The air-conditioned cab has four doors, two of which are on the rear side of the cab. (Photo courtesy Wayne Sorensen)

Washington State University at Pullman has its own fire department, and operates this 1992 KME 1,750-gpm pumper with a 500-gallon booster tank. (Photo courtesy Bill Hattersley)

Luverne became a major supplier to Chicago and, by 1994, there were 23 Spartan-Luverne pumpers on Chicago's roster, plus seven on order. They had 1,500-gpm pumps and 500-gallon water tanks. The Spartan cab tilts. This is Engine 15, a 1992 model. (Photo courtesy Bill Friedrich)

A 1992 Luverne running as Chicago's Engine 116 with a 1,500-gpm pump, 500-gallon water tank, and with a four-door cab. Note front mount suction. (Photo courtesy Bill Friedrich)

Elsmere, Delaware, runs this 1992 Pierce-Lance heavy-duty rescue unit. It carries a generator, winch, and rescue equipment. (Photo courtesy Ray Stevens)

Fairfield, California's Engine 10 is built on a 1992 Spartan chassis with a 1,250-gpm pump and 500-gallon water tank. In front of the turret is a loudspeaker that amplifies incoming radio messages. (Photo courtesy Bill Hattersley)

A 1992 Spartan Gladiator chassis with bodywork by Westates. This quadruple combination runs as Truck 2 for San Jose. The quad has a 1,500-gpm pump, 300-gallon water tank, and a 75-foot Tele-Squrt. This is the busiest truck in the San Jose Fire Department. (Photo courtesy Wayne Sorensen)

Portland, Oregon's Engine 9 is a 1992, 3-D 1,500-gpm pumper with a 500-gallon water tank and four-door cab. (Photo courtesy Bill Hattersley)

Arlington Heights, California, has in-service this 1992 Western States 1,250-gpm front-mount pumper with a 1,000-gallon water tank mounted on a Spartan chassis with a four-door cab. (Photo courtesy Bill Hattersley)

Portland, Oregon's Engine 18 runs this 1992 Western States 1,500-gpm pumper, equipped with a 500-gallon water tank, 100 gallons of foam, and a four-door cab. (Photo courtesy Bill Hattersley)

Paducah's Engine 1 is an Emergency One 1,250-gpm pumper built on Emergency One's "Protector" chassis. The pump is rated at 1,250-gpm and the booster tank carries 500 gallons. (Photo courtesy Dick Adelman)

Nashville's Engine 15 is the 1993 International, outfitted by Emergency One with a 1,250-gpm pump and 750-gallon booster tank. (Photo courtesy Dick Adelman)

Water Tanker 44 at Santa Cruz County at Loma Prieta, in California, has a 1,500-gpm pump with a 2,800-gallon water tank mounted by Westmark on a 1993 International chassis. Note the portable folding water tank carried on the side of tanker. (Photo courtesy Wayne Sorensen)

One of six 1993 Seagrave 100-foot rear-mount Patriot aerials purchased by Chicago. Power is from a Detroit diesel linked with an Allison transmission. Cab and bodies are of galvaneal steel. These are the first tilt-cab rear-mounts purchased by Chicago. (Photo courtesy Bill Friedrich)

Simon-LTI built this 106-foot aerial for Bellevue, Washington, in 1993. The cab has four doors. (Photo courtesy Bill Hattersley)

3-D Manufacturing built this engine for San Francisco on a 1992 Spartan chassis equipped with a 1,500-gpm pump, 500-gallon water tank, and four-door cab. (Photo courtesy Thom Taggart)

Corning, New York, uses this large 1992 American-LaFrance Century 2000 with a 2,000-gpm pump, a 200-gallon tank, and a 100-foot LTI tower ladder. (Photo courtesy Hattersley/Kadzielawski)

This is Saratoga, California's Hi-Tech 1,500-gpm pumper mounted on a Spartan chassis. The pumper carries 500 gallons of water and has a four-door stand-up cab. (Photo courtesy Wayne Sorensen)

A FDNY satellite hose tender with its five-inch deck pipe in use at a working fire. The unit was built by Saulsbury and mounted on a 1994 Mack MP chassis. (Photo courtesy Wayne Sorensen)

Cleveland, Ohio, runs this fully equipped 1994 Simon Duplex that carries a 2,000-gpm Waterous pump, a 150-gallon booster tank, and 188 feet of ground ladders. The Simon-LTI tower can handle a water flow of 2,000 gpm and carry a load of 1,000 pounds. (Photo courtesy Simon-LTI)

A 1994 Spartan Silent Knight-Hi-Tech hazardous materials spill response truck used in San Jose. Engine is mounted in the rear. (Photo courtesy Wayne Sorensen)

A 1994 Spartan Westates in-service at the Campbell Sunny Oaks Station of the Santa Clara Central Fire Protection District, in California. The unit has a 1,000-gpm pump and a 700-gallon water tank. It's owned by the state's Office of Emergency Services. The Fire Protection District has use of it but must have it and a crew available for use outside the district when needed. (Photo courtesy Wayne Sorensen)

The Santa Clara Central Fire Protection District, in California, runs this 1994 Spartan-Hi-Tech LTJ quintuple combination with a two-stage, 1,500-gpm pump, a 400-gallon tank, a 75-foot aerial ladder, and a Class A foam system. This foam system develops automatic proportions for the foam, and the foam has film-forming qualities. Power is provided by a Detroit diesel 8V-92 engine through an Allison World Transmission. Note roll-up compartment doors. The cab is air-conditioned. (Photo courtesy Wayne Sorensen)

A 100-foot tower ladder is on this 1994 Sutphen, used in Easton, Maryland. It also carries a 1,000-gpm pump. (Photo courtesy Ray Stevens)

Green Bay, Wisconsin, home of Super Bowl Champion XXXI Green Bay Packers, bought this 1994 custom pumper built by 3-D Manufacturing in nearby Shawano. The pump is a 1,250-gpm Hale and the chassis was supplied by Spartan. The top control panel is on an elevated walkway behind cab, and the truck carries a 750-gallon water tank. (Photo courtesy 3-D)

San Jose's Truck 18 is a Simon Duplex-LTI quint with a 75-foot, three-section, rear-mount ladder. It carries a 1,500-gpm Waterous pump. The large monitor can be operated from the raised ladder. The cab is air-conditioned. The powertrain consists of a Detroit diesel and an Allison transmission. (Photo courtesy Wayne Sorensen)

A rear quarter view of San Jose Truck 18. (Photo courtesy Wayne Sorensen)

A 1995 Spartan Hi-Tech pumper, one of eleven in-service at San Jose. The unit's cab is air-conditioned and it has a 1,500-gpm Hale pump and a 500-gallon booster tank. Shown is Engine 18. (Photo courtesy Wayne Sorensen)

Fallon/Churchill, Nevada, operates this three-axle Spartan/Darley. This massive truck carries a 1,500-gpm pump, a 2,250-gallon tank, 150 gallons of foam, and a 65-foot Tele-Squrt (shown extended). Automatic ladder racks lower ground ladders to be in reach of firefighters. The truck is shown at a drill tower. Note twin streams. (Unusual pattern on side of truck is shadow feeding through the ladder on the side rack.) (Photo courtesy Wayne Sorensen)

A body, built by Mobile Tech, Inc., was installed on a 1995 Ford "Cargo" tilt-cab chassis, powered by a Cummins diesel. It's equipped with a Ramsey winch and carries a large, mobile generator. High-intensity lights are installed on top of the body. It serves as Rescue 14 in Seattle. Graphics on the side of roll-up door show Seattle's skyline. (Photo courtesy Bill Hattersley)

San Jose's Truck 4 is a 1995 Simon-Duplex LTI. It has a 100-foot, rear-mount, four-section ladder with a waterway. The air-conditioned cab seats six. The powertrain includes a Detroit Diesel and an Allison World transmission. (Photo courtesy Wayne Sorensen)

Sacramento's 1995 Westates 1,500-gpm pumper with 500-gallon water tank mounted on a Spartan chassis with a four-door cab. (Photo courtesy Westates)

Casper, Wyoming's Engine 6 is on a 1996 HME chassis with bodywork by Becker. It has a 1,500-gpm pump and carries 1,000 gallons of water. (Photo courtesy Bill Hattersley)

Selected References

A Legend of Service: The History of the Elizabeth Fire Department (Elizabeth, NJ: the department, 1992).

Burgess-Wise, David. *Fire Engines & Fire Fighting,* (Norwalk, CT: Longmeadow Press, 1977).

Burks, John. *Working Fire—The San Francisco Fire Department,* (Mill Valley, CA: Squarebooks, 1982).

Calderone, John A. *A Guide to Boston Fire Apparatus* (Staten Island: Fire Apparatus Journal Publication, 1994).

———. *A Guide to New York City Fire Apparatus* (Staten Island: Fire Apparatus Journal Publication, 1990).

———, and Jack Lerch. *Wheels of the Bravest: A History of FDNY Fire Apparatus, 1865-1982,* (Howard Beach, NY: Fire Apparatus Journal Publications, 1984).

California Fire Service Directory (Sacramento: Eldon C. Nagel, 1994).

Cullom, Keith D. and Scott R. Miller. *Southern California Fire Service Directory* (Goleta, CA: Perfect Image, 1994).

Decker, Ralph and Clyde Talbert. *100 Years of Fire Fighting in the City of Destiny: Tacoma, Washington*, (Seattle: Grange Printing, 1981).

Ditzel, Paul C. *Fire Engines, Fire Fighters*, (New York: Rutledge Books, 1976).

Douglass, Emmons. *While the Flames Raged,* (Middletown, NY: 1993).

Eckart, Harvey. *Mack Fire Apparatus: A Pictorial History* (Middletown, NY: The Engine House, 1990).

Fire Apparatus Photo Album of the American-LaFrance 150th Anniversary, (Naperville, IL: The Visiting Fireman, 1982).

Fire Apparatus Photo Album of the Greenfield Village Musters, (Naperville, IL: The Visiting Fireman, 1984).

Fire Apparatus Photo Album of the Valhalla Musters, (Naperville, IL: The Visiting Fireman, 1983).

Freidrich, William and Mark Mitchell. *Chicago Fire Department Engines and Hook & Ladders, 1966-1995* (Deerfield, IL: Blitz Brothers Publications, 1995).

Goodenough, Simon. *Fire, The Story of the Fire Engine*, (Secaucus, NJ: Chartwell Books, 1978).

Goodman, M.W. *Inventing the American Fire Engine* (New Albany, Indiana: Fire Buff House Publishers, 1994).

Hagy, Steve. *Howe Fire Apparatus Album,* (Naperville, IL: The Visiting Fireman, 1984).

Halberstadt, Hans. *The American Fire Engine* (Osceola, WI: Motorbooks International, 1993).

Hart, Arthur A. *Fighting Fires on the Frontier*, (Boise, ID: Boise Fire Department Association, 1976).

Hashagen, Paul and Herb Eysser. *Fire Rescue: The History of FDNY Rescue Co. 1* (Staten Island: 1989).

Hass, Ed. *Ahrens-Fox, the Rolls Royce of Fire Engines*, (Sunnyvale, CA: the Author, 1982).

King, William T. *History of the American Fire Engine*, (Chicago: Owen Davies, 1960).

Klass, George. *Fire Apparatus: A Pictorial History of the Los Angeles Fire Department*, (Inglewood, CA: Mead, 1974).

Lee, Mathew. *A Pictorial History of Seagrave Fire Apparatus* (Kalamazoo: the author, 1991).

———. *Detroit Fire Department Apparatus History* (Kalamazoo: the author, 1989).

Malecky, John M. *Mack Tilt Cab Fire Apparatus* (Staten Island: Fire Apparatus Journal Publication, 1988).

Matches, Alex. *It Began with a Ronald*, (Vancouver, BC: the Author, 1974).

McCall, Walter. *American Fire Engines Since 1900*, (Glen Ellyn, IL: Crestline, 1976).

Nailen, Richard L. *Guardians of the Garden City, The History of the San Jose Fire Department*, (San Jose: Smith & McKay, 1972).

Salt Lake City Firemen's Relief Association, *A Pictorial History of the Salt Lake City Fire Department, 1871-1976*, (Salt Lake City: the Association, 1976).

Semanick, Murray. *Fire Engines* (New York: Crescent, 1992).

Sorensen, Wayne and Donald F. Wood. *Motorized Fire Apparatus of the West 1900-1906*, (Polo, IL: Transportation Trails, 1991).

Sytsma, John F. *Ahrens-Fox Album*, (Medino, OH: the Author, 1973).

———, and Robert Sams. *Ahrens-Fox, A Pictorial Tribute to a Great Name in Fire Apparatus*, (Medino, OH: the Author, 1971).

Weir, Dick. *Iron Men and Iron Machines* (Magnolia, Mass., 1976).

Wood, Donald F. and Wayne Sorensen. *American Volunteer Fire Trucks,* (Iola: Krause Publications, 1993).

Wren, James A. and Genevieve J. *Motor Trucks of America*,(Ann Arbor: The University of Michigan Press, 1979).

Also consulted were copies of company literature and catalogs, and of periodicals including *Fire Apparatus Journal, Engine! Engine!, Fire Service Digest, Fire Journal (Pacific Coast), Fire Engineering,* and *The American City.*

INDEX BY MANUFACTURER

A

Ahrens-Fox 6, 9–10, 34

American Fire Apparatus 9

American-LaFrance 12, 17, 20, 25, 34–35, 39, 47–49, 57–58, 63–64, 75, 86, 90, 94, 101, 109–110, 114, 123, 134–135, 142, 153, 158, 165–166, 184, 189, 200, 208, 223, 237, 262, 284, 302

Auto Body Works 10

Autocar 17, 21, 26, 41, 67, 184, 264

B

Barton 21, 132, 188

Beck 34, 217, 246, 293

Becker 327, 331

Boise Mobile Equipment Co. 291

Brockway 87

C

Central States Fire Apparatus Inc. 198

Chevrolet 124, 157, 168, 224, 247, 293

Corbitt 10

Crown Coach 291

Curtis, L.N., Co. 10, 55, 60, 100, 129, 138

Curtis-Heiser 45, 72, 106, 120

D

Darley 10, 19, 55, 217, 247, 291, 303, 305, 326, 329

Diamond T 11, 13, 22, 41, 46, 49, 70

Dodge 53–54, 64, 120, 122, 142, 190

Duplex 26, 32, 72, 85, 89, 93, 95, 102, 104, 108, 117, 129, 149, 155, 164, 211, 216, 231, 254–255, 261, 269, 282, 286, 319, 323, 328, 330

E

Emergency One 121, 147, 180, 198, 201, 209, 218–219, 224, 230, 237–238, 248, 264–265, 275, 291, 294–295, 304, 312–313, 320

F

Farrar Co. 291

FMC 179, 201, 209–210, 219, 225, 230–232, 238, 248, 250, 286

Ford 6, 10, 13, 44–45, 56, 58, 65, 77, 88, 91, 103, 111–112, 121–122, 124–125, 129, 135–136, 144–145, 153, 159, 163, 166, 179–180, 185, 191, 201, 210, 231–232, 239–240, 249, 254, 266–267, 273, 275, 296, 304–306, 320, 326, 330

Freightliner 202, 276, 291, 321, 327

FWD 10, 22, 31, 50, 55–56, 59, 69–71, 78, 88, 92, 96–97, 104, 122, 154, 156

G

General Safety Apparatus 121

GMC 8, 14, 18, 32, 42, 79, 112, 120–122, 197, 202, 306

H

Hahn Motors 56, 97, 113

Hale 6, 10–11, 15–16, 21, 23, 45, 65, 94, 113–114, 117, 121–122, 129, 180, 219, 265, 291, 295, 318, 321, 325, 329

Hall-Scott 11, 14, 23, 29–30, 49, 52, 66, 70, 72, 74, 95

Heiser 42, 45, 60, 72, 100, 106, 113–114, 130, 138, 160

Hendrickson 41, 121–122, 132, 137, 139, 145–146, 149–150, 155, 159, 162, 198, 209, 218

Hi-Tech Apparatus 273, 291, 307, 321–324, 329

HME 291, 331

Howe 18, 32, 136–137, 146–149, 161

I

Independent Truck Co. 120

International 6, 9–10, 14–15, 19, 24, 27, 30, 38, 41, 46, 54, 56, 59, 63, 73, 76, 80, 87, 105, 111, 120–121, 126, 130, 137–138, 167, 181, 191, 198, 220, 225, 231, 241, 244, 277, 291, 297–298, 313–314

J

Jacob Press 291

K

Kenworth 10–11, 15–16, 37, 65, 72, 106, 113–114, 130, 138, 160, 182, 232, 242

Kersey Manufacturing Co. 198

KME 241, 255, 267, 278–279, 299, 308, 327

L

LTI 122, 199, 216, 255, 260–261, 268–269, 280–282, 285, 287, 299, 301, 316, 321, 323, 328, 330

Luverne 291, 308–309

M

Mack 6, 10, 16, 19, 27, 34, 39, 42–43, 46, 53–54, 56, 81–84, 93, 98–99, 106–107, 115, 119–120, 122, 128, 131, 146–148, 156, 160–161, 192–195, 199, 204–205, 214, 221, 291, 314, 322

Magirus 10, 28, 39, 43

Marion Body Works 109, 291

Maxim 10, 28, 33, 55–56, 60–61, 69, 74, 84, 94, 100, 102–103, 110, 115, 122, 124, 138, 148, 162, 168, 186, 196, 199, 251, 256

Mobile Aerial Towers, Inc. 8

N

New Jersey Fire Equipment Corp. 36, 56, 104, 155

O

Oren-Roanoke 10, 56, 149
Oshkosh Truck 291, 300

P

Penfab 121, 198
Peterbilt 9, 23, 29–30, 37, 284, 300
Pierce 44, 88, 103, 105, 107, 132, 139, 145, 150, 162–163, 222, 252, 258, 266, 270, 285, 297, 301, 306, 309
Pierce-Arrow 122, 222, 243–244, 257–258, 285, 315
Pirsch 6, 10, 20, 24, 36, 40–41, 47, 56, 61, 75, 89, 91, 103, 112, 122, 125, 127, 131, 139, 150–151, 199, 206, 227, 232–234, 254
Pitman Manufacturing Co. 8, 10, 42, 55, 58, 71, 73, 75, 77, 92, 94, 139, 189, 250

R

Reo 41, 51

S

S & S Apparatus Co. 291
Salvage Corps 8, 54, 197
Sanford Motor Truck Co. 56, 80, 108
Saulsbury 131, 191, 199, 214, 234–235, 244, 256, 259, 271, 275–277, 291, 314, 318–319, 322
Seagrave 6, 9, 11, 24, 33, 38, 41, 52, 56, 62, 66, 85, 109, 114, 116, 122, 127–128, 133, 151–152, 156–157, 163, 182–183, 187–188, 199, 206, 213, 228–229, 235, 252, 259, 271–273, 291, 315–316, 318
Simon-LTI 199, 260, 286, 291, 316, 323, 328, 330
Smeal Apparatus 261, 291
Snorkel 44–45, 58, 66, 71, 73, 75, 77, 94, 120, 139, 184, 189, 199, 250
Spartan 195, 198, 201, 208–210, 215, 219, 234, 236, 246–249, 253, 259–261, 271, 276, 280, 282, 287–288
Steeldraulic Products 199, 242

Super Vac 220, 253, 291, 314
Sutphen 32, 52, 56, 122, 140, 145, 152, 199, 207, 216, 223, 245, 287, 291, 301, 325

T

3-D 168, 210, 269, 288, 291, 311, 317, 325–326
Tele-Squrt 54, 124, 139, 141–143, 151, 190, 194, 222, 240, 276, 310, 329
Towers Fire Apparatus Co. 56, 291

U

Utah LaGrange, Inc. 291

V

Van Pelt 8, 11, 15–16, 49, 56, 65–66, 70, 89, 101, 117, 121, 164, 198, 216, 219, 225, 230, 238, 291
Volvo/White 21, 67

W

Ward LaFrance 6, 8–9, 11–12, 17, 20, 25, 34–35, 39, 47–49, 55–57, 62–64, 67, 75, 86, 90, 94, 101, 109–110, 114, 118–120, 122–123, 133–135, 141–142, 153, 158, 164–166, 177, 184, 189, 196–198, 200, 208, 223, 237, 262, 283–284, 292
Warner and Swasey Co. 10
Waterous 11, 14–15, 22, 29, 46, 58, 64, 76, 80, 87, 105, 121–122, 252, 291, 323, 328
Westates 11, 122, 124, 137–138, 167, 183, 185, 199, 202, 241, 289, 291, 304, 310, 319, 324, 331
Western States Fire Apparatus 122
Westmark 262, 291

Y

Young Fire Equipment Corp. 13, 291

Z

Zabek Fire Apparatus 10

CALL FOR BACKUP
and seize the BEST auto books on wheels!

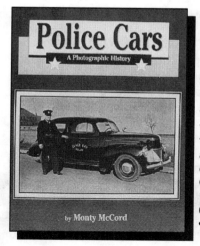

Police Cars: A Photographic History Take a complete pictorial history tour of police vehicles through the ages with author Monty McCord – from the horse drawn paddy wagons to the latest technologically advanced, laser-equipped "Corvette Cops" of the 1990s. 8-1/2x11 SC • 304p • 600+ photos • **PC01 $14.95**

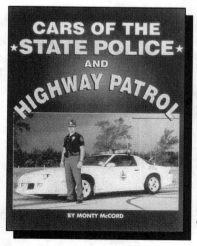

Cars of the State Police and Highway Patrol arms you with an in-depth photographic look at the vehicles, past and present, used by America's state police agencies. Monty McCord shows you close-up photos of door markings and license plates. 8-1/2x11 SC • 304p • 500 photos • **CSP01 $16.95**

Trucking in America – Moving the Goods delivers a concise, informative and detailed photo-history of how the highway haulers of yesterday forged the American economy of today. John Gunnell includes hundreds of rare photos showing you all kinds of trucks from yesteryear. 8-1/2x11 SC • 304p • 500 photos • **ATR01 $16.95**

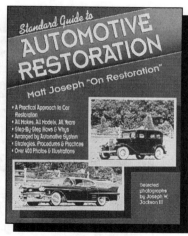

Standard Guide to Automotive Restoration will help you complete your restoration project with over 500 photos and step-by-step instructions. Matt Joseph explains carburetion, electrical, body and paint, engine mechanical and more! 8-1/2x11 SC • 384p • 560 photos • **AJ01 $24.95**

I'm in pursuit! Give me the following books:

Qty.	Title	Price	Total
	Police Cars: A Photographic History	$14.95	
	Cars of the State Police and Highway Patrol	$16.95	
	Trucking in America – Moving the Goods	$16.95	
	Standard Guide to Automotive Restoration	$24.95	

Shipping: $3.25 1st book, $2.00 each additional. WI residents please add 5.5% sales tax. IL residents add 7.75% sales tax. Outside U.S. add $10.00 for 1st book, $5.00 each additional. (Canadian orders shipped air parcel post, all others via book post).	Subtotal	
	Shipping	
	Tax	
	TOTAL	

Name _____

Address _____

City _____

State _____ Zip _____

Phone ( ) _____

❏ Check or money order enclosed (payable to Krause Publications)
❏ Visa ❏ MasterCard ❏ Discover ❏ American Express

Card # _____

Expires: Mo./Yr. _____

Signature _____

mail with payment to:

Krause Publications, Dept. ZQB2
700 E. State St., Iola, WI 54990-0001

Credit card customers call toll-free
800-258-0929 Dept. ZQB2
M-F: 7 a.m. - 8 p.m., Sat.: 8 a.m. - 2 p.m.

S T E P ON IT!

And answer the call to great auto books!

BIG CITY FIRE TRUCKS
VOLUME 1 • 1900-1950

• More than 500 photos for identification
• Complete technical specs
• Unusual and unique trucks and equipment

Donald F. Wood &

New

AMERICAN VOLUNTEER FIRE TRUCKS

By Donald F. Wood & Wayne Sorensen

THE ILLUSTRATED ENCYCLOPEDIA OF AMERICAN TRUCKS AND COMMERCIAL VEHICLES

• Over 1,240 makes
• More than 1,000 illust.
• Cross-referenced for obscure makes
Albert Mroz • Covers 1891-1996

New

Big City Fire Trucks, 1900-1950, Volume I, calls out the monster trucks, exotic equipment and unique apparatus of professional departments. Donald F. Wood and Wayne Sorensen include year of manufacture, make of truck chassis, commercial outfitter and equipment for each listing. 8-1/2x11 SC • 336p • 500 photos • **BCF01 $18.95**

American Volunteer Fire Trucks Wood & Sorenson provide you with a pictorial history of over 500 rigs used by volunteer fire departments across America. Fire trucks often referred to as "brush rigs," are all built on commercial chassis with fire-fighting equipment added. 8-1/2x11 SC • 336p • 500+ photos • **FT01 $16.95**

The Illustrated Encyclopedia of American Trucks & Commercial Vehicles drives you through a special segment of vehicle industry, 1891-1996. Find 1,240 makes, unusual prototypes, major manufacturers explained by auto expert Albert Mroz. 8-1/2x11 SC • 432p • 1,350 photos • **AWT01 $34.95**

I'm answering the call! Please send me:

Qty.	Title	Price	Total
	Big City Fire Trucks	$18.95	
	American Volunteer Fire Trucks	$16.95	
	The Illustrated Encyclopedia of American Trucks & Commercial Vehicles	$34.95	

Shipping: $3.25 1st book, $2.00 each additional. WI residents please add 5.5% sales tax. IL residents add 7.75% sales tax. Outside U.S. add $10.00 for 1st book, $5.00 each additional. (Canadian orders shipped air parcel post, all others via book post).	**Subtotal**
	Shipping
	Tax
	TOTAL

Credit card customers call toll-free

800-258-0929 Dept. ZQB1

M-F: 7 a.m. - 8 p.m., Sat.: 8 a.m. - 2 p.m.

Name _____

Address _____

City _____

State _____ Zip _____

Phone ( ) _____

❑ Check or money order enclosed (payable to Krause Publications)

❑ Visa ❑ MasterCard ❑ Discover ❑ American Express

Card # _____

Expires: Mo./Yr. _____

Signature _____

mail with payment to:

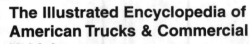

Krause Publications, Dept. ZQB1
700 E. State St., Iola, WI 54990-0001